Practical...Profound...A loving g ....e for those who are lost or searching for answers. Bollinger writes with conviction, compassion, and humility *Don't All Roads Lead to God?* is a timely and accessible roadmap that warns of the pitfalls of following the broad road of contemporary culture while welcoming the reader to true purpose and meaning found only in Christ.

—CHARLIE KIRK,

Founder and President, Turning Point USA

Wow! Debbie Bollinger has done it again: written a road map for life that safely delivers the reader to God's throne of power and grace. Debbie's handbook is an easy reference guide you will return to again and again to answer the common lies of the enemy with the truth that sets us free. Reading *Don't All Roads Lead to God* is like having a cold bucket of water thrown on your face that quickly turns into a warming tonic for your soul. It's a powerful work that awakens the reader to the insidious and dangerous lies of the enemy and transports us to positions of truth, power and peace. Keep a copy on your night stand, in your office, and in your car and you will always be ready to help direct people through the mosh pits of life to firm ground—and it will also help you find your own way when you find yourself lost or confused.

—REBECCA HAGELIN,

former CEO United in Purpose

Our human propensity is to take the path of least resistance, look for the easy answers and to remain mentally lazy and spiritually ignorant. This book will challenge you with hard questions, and you will have to think and then you will have to choose! DL Bollinger's second installment of RTR will gently but ever so firmly pull you from your moral slumber and challenge you with the Truth of God's Word. In a global culture that has all but dismissed a God who is both Loving and Holy, this book will bring us face to face with the One True God who has revealed Himself to us through His Son, Jesus Christ. This is certainly a "whosoever will" book, everyone should read it and think through the issues presented and be ready to choose Jesus.

—DR. MARTI WILLIAMS

Over the years, my wife, Debbie, and I have become good friends with Debbie Bollinger, and we are excited to recommend her new book, *Rabbit Trails Redirect: Don't All Roads Lead to God?* In this timely book, she compares issues in today's culture to the truth of God's Word, and I know you'll find it refreshing. I hope this book will be a blessing to you and strengthen your passion for the Lord in today's tumultuous times.

—ROBERT MORRIS, Senior Pastor, Gateway Church,
Bestselling Author of *The Blessed Life*,
Beyond Blessed, and *Take the Day Off*

Our culture and our country are so confused, deceived and in disarray. People need the truth. Debbie Bollinger's book is so needed and timely. The truth is always the narrow road, because it excludes all the false roads; but the truth brings freedom.

—KELLY SHACKELFORD,
President/CEO First Liberty Institute

In a world where influencer voices and countless opinions have a me-centered, feelings-driven approach to the study of Scripture, Debbie is passionate about leading us back to God's Voice of Truth. She inspires me to clear the fog in my mind and heart when it comes to studying God's Word and apply it to the issues the world is navigating today!

—AMY FORD,
Speaker, Author and Founder of Embrace Grace

This is a Clarion to awaken us to our current state, and cries out for a response. As adults we have surrendered our privilege to think, feel, and choose, to others. This book clarifies that image of God in which we are created, in that we have a mind, will, and emotions. It's time to choose LIFE and reclaim that image. Thanks Debbie for calling us out from our slumber, to integrity.

—LARRY ADLEY,
Director Fort Worth Women's Teen Challenge

Don't All Roads Lead to God? is a 21ˢᵗ century Francis Schaeffer, C.S. Lewis, *Pilgrim's Progress* book that every God-fearing Christian must read. Having known Glenn and Debbie Bollinger for decades, I realize they have walked the talk and lived out the principles in this masterpiece.

—MIKE EVANS,

#1 *New York Times* bestselling author

It was John the Apostle who wrote near the end of his gospel, "I've written all these things so that you would fall in love with the one who has captured my heart". It is so obvious as one journeys to the center of this book that the author of *Rabbit Trails Redirect Vol 2* has the same heart and hope. This is a book of love for Jesus and grace for the reader. While dealing with the most difficult questions—it is truth that wins, yet mercy is the champion. Perhaps the core message of DL Bollinger's wonderful book is found deep within the pages when the author writes, "God is a God of inclusion not exclusion!" Make sure you get the printed copy. It is a book to mark up, to write one's own notes in … to purchase several for friends and loved ones. Thank the Lord for writers that are willing to do the hard work that will deeply set the anchor of God's truth for a culture adrift in the chaos of compromise.

—DR. PAUL LOUIS COLE,

President, Christian Men's Network

Some things need to be heard. Hard things. Controversial things. Eternal things. In a continuation of her first book, Debbie Bollinger confronts the issues of our generation and the road signs that push us in many different and deceptive directions. The prophetic cry of her heart points us to the one and only way: a genuine relationship with Jesus Christ. Open your heart and settle in with a cup of coffee, RTR will challenge and inspire you.

—STEPHEN EVANS,
Evangelical leader

I read only a few books with a highlighter in hand, and this is one of them. If you like reading Mark Levin, Glenn Beck, or Dinesh D'Souza, you will love reading D.L. Bollinger. The author investigates material in a way that brings out unique distinctions and connections you would have otherwise missed. In a world of disinformation, there will likely be a competing deluge of conspiracy theories seeking to make sense of it all. D.L. Bollinger has given us a great gift in providing a book that navigates us through this blizzard of competing narratives. Bollinger connects the dots by filtering data through the lens of transcendent faith. This book forms a clear picture. It explains not only what has happened, but what is happening now, and what is likely to come next. Make this book a priority.

—LANCE WALLNAU, Best Selling Author,
Teacher, Media Personality

RABBIT TRAILS REDIRECT

DON'T ALL ROADS LEAD TO GOD?

VOLUME TWO

D.L. BOLLINGER

DIVINE ORIGIN PRESS

P.O. Box 3440, Grapevine, Texas 76099

RABBIT TRAILS REDIRECT

VOLUME TWO

When it comes to the most controversial, divisive, and polarizing topics we deal with as a society today, what does the Bible actually have to say regarding each topic? Are we misinformed? Are we parroting the politically correct dogma we've been brainwashed to believe through education, media, and culture?

Don't All Roads Lead to God? leads those searching for spiritual clarity, back to the Word of God for answers. Whether Jew or Gentile, Christian or atheist, Believer or unbeliever, this book is not only for those who have never read the Bible from cover to cover, but for every hungry soul seeking the wisdom and truth given to us *only* by our Creator.

Don't All Roads Lead to God? was written as a helpful, abbreviated topical reference guide for anyone in need of quick Biblical references regarding a certain controversial topic and shines a bright light on the path leading to Truth.

Rabbit Trails Redirect is dedicated

to my husband Glenn,

my children Branson, Joy, Brendon, Meredith, Lacey,

my grandchildren Ronan Hart, Cora Bourne,

Waylynn Marie, Callaway Wright, Heston Dell

and to all those precious ones who follow.

There is no greater legacy I can leave behind

than to point the way to the path of Truth

found only in God's Word, the Bible.

— CHAPTER SIX —

We stumble and fall chasing deceptive

false promises of pleasure, fulfillment,

spirituality, and convenience,

as we blindly follow every rabbit trail

that offers to satisfy our selfish,

hedonistic, sensibilities of self.

DO ALL ROADS LEAD TO GOD?

"But we don't want to hear warnings today.
We only want positive words. Words that make us
feel better about ourselves. Words that increase
our self-esteem and enhance our self-image.
Anything negative will be rejected out of hand.
Don't tell me I'm on the wrong path. Don't tell me
there's danger ahead."

—DR. MICHAEL L BROWN

There are many in the world who see spirituality and religion as a giant road map with multi-lane Interstate Highways, city streets, farm roads, and dirt paths. . .all leading to God. The thinking is no matter which road we choose or the compass we use for direction, we still end up in the same place. In other words, to them, there are no wrong choices.

If true, that sounds lovely. If it's not, it would be like using a road map for Los Angeles when we need directions in Dallas. We're not going to end up where we need to be, and ultimately we will be horribly lost. If this is true, then what are the choices? How do we navigate the potholes, roadblocks, detours, accidents, slippery roads, dangerous slowdowns, and the inevitable dead end? Which roads do we have to choose from to get to our destination? Better yet, where can we find the proper coordinates to program our Global Positioning System (GPS)?

Thanks to modern technology, many of us have replaced our road maps with a GPS that uses satellite-based navigational technology. For any good GPS to be effective, you have to factor in two coordinates: your starting position and your final destination. Most people, when asked, would say they would like heaven to be their final destination. The Bible tells us there is a physical Heaven and Hell, and we will ultimately end up in one or the other, based on our choices in this life. If Heaven is your ultimate goal and desired final destination, then it becomes necessary to determine your starting point.

Which road are you on right now? Is it the broad road, which can disguise itself as a variety of different thoroughfares such as: the seemingly good road, the crooked road, the divided road, or perhaps the extremely deceptive and crowded open road? Hopefully, you are traveling the narrow road the Bible tells us will lead to eternal Life. Let's check the coordinates to see if a course correction is necessary.

"YOUR WORD
IS A LAMP
TO GUIDE MY FEET
AND A LIGHT
FOR MY PATH."

—PSALM 119:105 NLT

CHAPTER ONE:

THE BROAD ROAD

WE CRUISE
THROUGH LIFE
WITH A
FLAWED LOGIC
THINKING WE'RE
IN CONTROL.

1

THE BROAD ROAD

"Enter through the narrow gate. For wide is the gate
and broad is the road that leads to destruction,
and many enter through it. But small is the gate and
narrow the road that leads to life and only a few find it"
(Mathew 7:13, NIV).

L ogical thinking would tell us truth and deception are miles apart. In reality, they're not distant at all, but running in the same direction and almost parallel—at least at first. Satan deals in deception, it's his forte. Therefore, it's no coincidence the broad road and the narrow road would each be in the same vicinity. How much easier for him to deceive this way.

The enemy, who is out to steal our soul, is adept at offering a counterfeit for everything God offers. 2 Corinthians 11:14–15 states, "And no wonder! For Satan disguises himself as an angel of light. So it is no great surprise if his servants also disguise themselves as servants of righteousness. Their end will be according to their works" (CSB).

What is this broad road with a wide gate to which the Bible is referring? It would be more obvious and certainly helpful if it were heading in the opposite direction of the narrow road. Yes, deception would undoubtedly be more identifiable if marked with skull and crossbones or a tail and a pitchfork; however, the broad road is more subtle. If the narrow road referred to in Scripture leads to the Kingdom of heaven, then the broad road with its convenience of multiple lanes, high speed, and roadside entertainment, unfortunately, deceives and transports the masses to the ultimate dead end. "Don't be misled—you cannot mock the justice of God. You will always harvest what you plant. Those who live only to satisfy their own sinful nature will harvest decay and death from that sinful nature. But those who live to please the spirit will harvest everlasting life from the Spirit" (Galatians 6:7–8, NLT).

THE DECEPTION OF CRUISE CONTROL

How do we end up on the broad road of life? Do we make a conscious choice to travel the Interstate, rather than the road less traveled? This is the case for some, but most likely we find ourselves negotiating the broad road along with the rest of the traffic because we made no choice at all. We simply "go along to get along," looking for the path of least resistance to get through our harried lives and hectic schedules. And who wouldn't want to choose the easiest route with the most exciting options?

We cruise through life with a flawed logic thinking we're in control. We keep our eyes on our #1 goal of immediate, short-term risk avoidance, all the while dangerously gambling with our long-term destination of eternal security. Our temporal existence on earth involves our inhabiting a shell made in God's image that comprises a spirit, soul, and a body. All three need care, maintenance, and refueling regularly.

We tend to prioritize the physical attention grabbers, the mental instant gratification fillers, and the emotional self-esteem and ego builders, leaving little to no time for our spiritual batteries to be recharged. Instead of living intentional lives of purpose, we spend our days coasting along, putting out fires, and focusing on what is shouting the loudest for our attention. We are easily deceived and sidetracked because of the absence of a Divinely charted course.

SCRIPTURE REFERENCES:

"This man will come to do the work of Satan with counterfeit power and signs and miracles. He will use every kind of evil deception to fool those on their way to destruction, because they refuse to love and accept the truth that would save them" (2 Thessalonians 2:9–10, NLT).

"My goal is that they may be encouraged in heart and united in love, so that they may have the full riches of complete understanding, in order that they may know the mystery of God, namely, Christ, in whom are hidden all the treasures of wisdom and knowledge. I tell you this so that no one may deceive you by fine-sounding arguments" (Colossians 2:2–4, NIV)

"I say this because many deceivers have gone out into the world. They deny that Jesus Christ came in a real body. Such a person is a deceiver and an antichrist" (2 John 1:7, NLT).

"Jesus answered: 'Watch out that no one deceives you. For many will come in my name, claiming, I am the Christ, and will deceive many. For as lightning that comes from the east is visible even in the west, so will be the coming of the Son of Man'" (Mathew 24:4–5 and 27, NIV).

"Let no one deceive you with empty words, for because of such things God's wrath comes on those who are disobedient. Therefore do not be partners with them" (Ephesians 5:6–7, NIV).

"IF WE SAY WE HAVE NO SIN, WE DECEIVE OURSELVES, AND THE TRUTH IS NOT IN US"

—1 JOHN 1:8, NKJV

MAKING A CONSCIOUS CHOICE

Throughout His Word and His commandments, God's loving objective is to provide clear direction and to warn His children not to be deceived. Without making a conscious choice to seek the truth of God, we make an unconscious choice to detour from the truth. Slipping into cruise control, we get swept up into the heavy traffic flowing down the broad road. Before we know it, we've become accustomed to being hemmed in on all sides, letting those around us who are larger, louder, or moving faster determine our direction. After a while, it becomes easier just to stay with the flow than to entertain the idea of trying to exit the busy highway for a less traveled road. With the radio and road noise drowning out any other sound, many spend their entire lives in this mode of "highway hypnosis," spiritually asleep at the wheel.

The broad road can branch out, subtly changing directions and appearing with many forms and surfaces, transporting us to various and exciting adventures and getaway experiences. None of these will lead us to the *Ultimate Divine Destination* of spending eternity with our Creator and Savior. Without purposely programing our spiritual GPS toward Jesus, which leads to eternity in heaven, we most likely have been detoured onto a thoroughfare that is taking us not only in the wrong direction, but ultimately leads to destruction.

"Yet God has made everything beautiful for its own time. He has planted eternity in the human heart, but even so, people cannot see the whole scope of God's work from beginning to end (Ecclesiastes 3:11, NLT).

"The King will reply, 'Truly I tell you, whatever you did for one of the least of these brothers and sisters of mine, you did for me.' Then he will say to those on his left, 'Depart from me, you who are cursed, into the eternal fire prepared for the devil and his angels. For I was hungry and you gave me nothing to eat, I was thirsty and you gave me nothing to drink, I was a stranger and you did not invite me in, I needed clothes and you did not clothe me, I was sick and in prison and you did not look after me.' They also will answer, 'Lord, when did we see you hungry or thirsty or a stranger or needing clothes or sick or in prison, and did not help you?' He will reply,

'Truly I tell you, whatever you did not do for one of the least of these, you did not do for me.' Then they will go away to eternal punishment, but the righteous to eternal life" (Matthew 25:40–46, NIV).

Are we traveling one of these roads? See if any of the landscape looks familiar?

WITHOUT MAKING
A CONSCIOUS CHOICE
TO SEEK THE
TRUTH OF GOD,
WE MAKE AN
UNCONSCIOUS
CHOICE TO DETOUR
FROM THE TRUTH.

CHAPTER TWO:

THE

GOOD

ROAD

IN THE ECONOMY
OF GOD, THE CONSTANT
STRIVING TO BE GOOD
WILL NEVER BE GOOD
ENOUGH. WE WERE NOT
CREATED WITH THE
ABILITY TO PERFORM
SELF-SALVATION.

2

THE GOOD ROAD

Surveys show a high percentage of people believe that if they're good, or at least try to do the right things most of the time, they will go to heaven. They might say, "I'm a good person. I believe in God. I give to charity. I pay my taxes. I obey the laws. I go to church or mass. I work hard and pay my bills. I teach a Sunday school class. I've never been arrested. I signed a card and walked down the aisle at church. I'm a seminary professor. I volunteer at a soup kitchen. I'm a member of the clergy. I'm a good neighbor. I'm involved with a ministry. I've gone through Bible School or catechism, and I've attended intensive retreats or Bible classes. I go on mission trips to areas of need. I give regularly to starving children in Africa.

I started a charitable foundation." This all sounds good to me, but what if it takes more than sending a check, joining a church, teaching a class, or staying out of jail? Proverbs 14:12 reads, "There is a way that seems right to a person, but its end is the way to death (CSB).

Barna Survey: Slightly over half of Christian respondents said they believe someone can attain salvation by "being or doing good," a figure that includes 46% of Pentecostals, 44% of mainline Protestants, 41% of evangelicals, and 70% of Catholics.

—GEORGE BARNA

Can we trust our feelings, emotions, education, or even our intellect to make such a life and death decision? Have we sought the truth for ourselves? Alternatively, are we merely being transported down the long-established and well-traveled surfaces of a generational familial culture, public opinion, or post-modern political correctness? What type of guidance does the Bible give?

"IF YOU DON'T KNOW WHERE YOU'RE GOING—ANY ROAD WILL TAKE YOU THERE."

—ANONYMOUS

SCRIPTURE REFERENCES:

"All Scripture is inspired by God and is useful to teach us what is true and to make us realize what is wrong in our lives. It corrects us when we are wrong and teaches us to do what is right" (2 Timothy 3:16 , NLT).

"Jesus answered, "I am the way and the truth and the life. No one comes to the Father except through me" (John 14:6, NIV).

"The Lord is my light and my salvation; Whom shall I fear? The Lord is the strength of my life; Of whom shall I be afraid?" (Psalms 27:1, NKJV).

"I will instruct you and show you the way to go; with my eye on you I will give counsel" (Psalm 32:8, CSB).

"I will lead the blind by ways they have not known, along unfamiliar paths I will guide them; I will turn the darkness into light before them and make the rough places smooth. These are the things I will do; I will not forsake them" (Isaiah 42:16, NIV).

"A person's steps are established by the Lord, and he takes pleasure in his way" (Psalm 37:23, CSB).

"Don't be afraid, for I am with you. Don't be discouraged, for I am your God. I will strengthen you and help you. I will hold you up with my victorious right hand" (Isaiah 41:10, NLT).

"IN HIS HEART A MAN PLANS HIS COURSE, BUT THE LORD DETERMINES HIS STEPS."

—PROVERBS 16:9, NIV

IN THE HABIT OF DOING GOOD

A ministry in which I have served on their Board for many years, has enriched my life far more than I could have ever given in return. Through the years, I've witnessed the godly director of this ministry and the administrative staff, along with many volunteers, who faithfully gave of their time and treasure to support what God was doing in this ministry. As a result, hundreds of precious lives that were damaged, addicted, thrown away, and considered hopeless by the world, are now living victorious lives of miraculous spiritual and physical healing, with many experiencing healthy marriages and families of their own.

When I think of someone sacrificing their life by earnestly striving to do good, one of this ministries' full-time staff of many years comes to mind. At an early age, Mary's tender heart for God led her to become a Nun. She diligently served God with all her heart in every area that she was placed. Over time, she increasingly felt God was calling her out of the Convent. It was after leaving the Convent that she asked Jesus into her heart as her Lord and Savior and found her way to this ministry.

This came as a great shock to me. Not that others who live in a Convent or who have given their life in complete devotion and service to God aren't a Christian or don't have a personal relationship with Jesus! This is Mary's story, with the point being, that she spent many years in devoted service to God being a very good person and yet according to the Bible (obedience to God's Word is the only thing that counts for eternity), Mary was unfortunately standing next to God's umbrella of eternal blessing, not under it and was missing the Salvation provided by Jesus' cleansing blood.

> "Not everyone who says to me, 'Lord, Lord,' will enter the kingdom of heaven, but the one who does the will of my Father who is in heaven. On that day many will say to me, 'Lord, Lord, did we not prophesy in your name, and cast out demons in your name, and do many mighty works in your name? And then will I declare to them, 'I never knew you; depart from me, you workers of lawlessness" (Matthew 7:21–23, ESV).

What is the will of God? That everyone on earth would accept His Son! In the economy of God, the constant striving by mankind to be good will never be good enough. We were not created with the ability to perform self-salvation. Only Jesus, God's Son, and sinless Savior, could perform such an indescribable act of selfless love for His Creation. Being good is its own reward, but will never be the key to unlocking the entrance to our eternal security. Luke 19:10 reads, "For the Son of Man has come to seek and to save the lost" (CSV).

A person who invites Jesus to take up residence in their heart, experiences the exhilaration of being found by the Lord of Lords and King of the universe, receiving goodness and so much more straight from the Source! We are then reconciled back to our heavenly Father because we have chosen His beloved Son. This is the only way alignment with our heavenly Father is possible. It's as if He's holding a giant umbrella of blessings flowing down to His children, but only those who have chosen Jesus, will be obediently positioned in alignment under this divine umbrella and experience His Salvation, blessing, favor, provision, and eternal life.

"So we praise God for the glorious grace he has poured out on us who belong to his dear Son. He is so rich in kindness and grace that he purchased our freedom with the blood of his Son and forgave our sins. He has showered his kindness on us, along with all wisdom and understanding. God has now revealed to us his mysterious plan regarding Christ, a plan to fulfill his own good pleasure. And this is the plan: At the right time he will bring everything together under the authority of Christ—everything in heaven and on earth" (Ephesians 1:6–10, NLT).

A lifetime spent doing good things, obeying the laws, paying your taxes, volunteering at your child's school or a local charity, taking care of your neighbors, giving to worthy causes, but not accepting Jesus into your heart, is by far the most heart-breaking decision one could make in this life! Choosing to stand away from God's umbrella of eternal blessing and security, or even standing near or right next to it, will end up being "a near miss," leaving a spiritually fruitless and temporal legacy that dies with us. Choose eternal Life. Choose Jesus!

WHAT IS THE WILL OF GOD? THAT EVERYONE ON EARTH WOULD ACCEPT HIS SON!

CHAPTER THREE:

THE

CROOKED

ROAD

FOR EVERY
BLESSING GOD
HAS FOR US,
THE ENEMY
HAS DEVISED A
COUNTERFEIT.

3

THE CROOKED ROAD

"Let the wicked change their ways
and banish the very thought of doing wrong.
Let them turn to the Lord that he may
have mercy on them. Yes, turn to our God,
for he will forgive generously"
(Isaiah 55:7, NLT).

Every time, Satan's method of choice is deception! For every blessing God has for us, the enemy has devised a counterfeit. We don't just awaken one morning in the middle of immorality and depravity. As with the frog in the pot of boiling water, the water heated gradually with little notice until he was boiled alive. One bad choice after another and before you know it, perhaps you have found yourself in a place you never planned to be.

There's a saying, "Sin takes you places you never intended to go, makes you do things you never intended to do, keeps you longer than you intended to stay, and costs you more than you ever intended to pay." Sin is a downward spiral, one step leading to the next, making it difficult to stop until you've hit bottom. Is there a depth to which God can no longer reach us? Is there a place we can hide where we are out of his sight? Jeremiah 23:23–24 states, "Am I only a God nearby," declares the Lord, "and not a God far away? Who can hide in secret places so that I cannot see them?" declares the Lord. "Do not I fill heaven and earth?" declares the Lord" (NIV).

REPENTANCE BRINGS FREEDOM

God does not regard traveling on the crooked road of sin as a point of no return. Grace, mercy, and forgiveness are demonstrated throughout His Word in the Bible and are lovingly made available to anyone who repents of their sins. This allows God to redirect their path. However, there is an extremely deceptive undercurrent flowing through many churches today, undermining the need for repentance for our sins both before and after salvation. It attaches itself to the amazing gift of grace we have received from the priceless blood Jesus shed on the cross for our sins. Some claim that because of this grace, the need to repent is no longer necessary. Let's hear what God's Word has to say about the need for repentance and forgiveness.

SCRIPTURE REFERENCES

Mathew 4:17 "From that time on Jesus began to preach, "Repent, for the kingdom of heaven has come near." (NIV)

Mark 6:12 "So the disciples went out, telling everyone they met to repent of their sins and turn to God." (NLT)

Luke 13:2-3 "Do you think those Galileans were worse sinners than all the other people from Galilee?" Jesus asked. "Is that why they suffered? Not at all! And you will perish, too, unless you repent of your sins and turn to God." (NLT)

Acts 2:38 "Peter replied, "Each of you must repent of your sins and turn to God, and be baptized in the name of Jesus Christ for the forgiveness of your sins. Then you will receive the gift of the Holy Spirit." (NLT)

> "GOD OVERLOOKED PEOPLE'S IGNORANCE ABOUT THESE THINGS IN EARLIER TIMES, BUT NOW HE COMMANDS EVERYONE EVERYWHERE TO REPENT OF THEIR SINS AND TURN TO HIM."
>
> —ACTS 17:30 NLT

God's divine intent in His Holy Word is not vague or indiscernible. He created us with a free will and knows that the act of repentance enables us to surrender our will to His completely, allowing His Spirit to transform our hearts and minds. God in His infinite grace and mercy carefully gives instruction in His Holy Word, so that every man, woman, boy, and girl can be reconciled to Him through His Son. He has already done the hard work of buying us back from the clutches of eternal damnation, through the blood Jesus willingly shed in our place. All we have to do is repent and receive this priceless gift of salvation. Our Heavenly Father lovingly warns us not to be reckless with this precious gift and to be vigilant to guard our hearts from the deceptions of Satan. What does God's Word have to say about repentance and forgiveness *after* salvation?

SCRIPTURE REFERENCES

Revelation 2:5 "Consider how far you have fallen! Repent and do the things you did at first. If you do not repent, I will come to you and remove your lampstand from its place." (NIV)

1 Timothy 4:1-2 "The Spirit clearly says that in later times some will abandon the faith and follow deceiving spirits and things taught by demons. Such teachings come through hypocritical liars, whose consciences have been seared as with a hot iron. (NIV)

2 Peter 2:20-21 "If they have escaped the corruption of the world by knowing our Lord and Savior Jesus Christ and are again entangled in it and overcome, they are worse off at the end than they were at the beginning. It would have been better for them not to have known the way of righteousness, than to have known it and then to turn their backs on the sacred command that was passed on to them." (NIV)

1 John 1:9-10 "If we confess our sins, He is faithful and just to forgive us our sins and to cleanse us from all unrighteousness. If we say that we have not sinned, we make Him a liar, and His word is not in us. (NKJV)

Our Heavenly Father teaches His children in His Word how to walk in faith, freedom, and victory. He wants us to not only have life but to have it more abundantly. He knows that for us to walk in an intimate relationship with Jesus, as our Lord and Savior, we must be willing to daily confess and ask forgiveness for our sins and to submit *our* will in obedience to the cross of Christ. John 10:10 reads, "The thief does not come except to steal, and to kill, and to destroy. I have come that they may have life, and that they may have it more abundantly" (NKJV).

THE DICHOTOMIES OF GOD

The hidden treasures of the Bible are found in His Divine dichotomies that call us to walk in sanctified excellence; the process by which the fire of the Holy Spirit sets us apart and makes us vessels of righteousness and holiness to carry His presence. These are spiritual principles that are completely foreign to our carnal nature and can only be spiritually discerned through faith in God's Word. Interestingly, they require us to do exactly the opposite of what feels right, natural, and what our fleshly desires and common sense are telling us to do; therefore, setting His children apart because of their uncompromising obedience to His Word

- Only in sincere *repentance* can we experience the joy of Salvation.

- Only in complete *surrender* can we experience our divine Destiny.

- Only in Biblical *obedience* can we experience true Celebration.

- Only in *humility* can we experience true Promotion.

- Only in *generosity of spirit* can we experience true Abundance.

- Only in *forgiving others* can we experience total Freedom.

"Excellence is a Kingdom value and is not to be confused with perfectionism which is a counterfeit and comes from the religious spirit.
One of the clearest paths of promotion is through excellence. God is speaking to prophets to call the modern-day Church to rise up and to awaken."

—LANCE WALLNAU,
author *Invading Babylon: The 7 Mountain Mandate*

OFFENCES CAN BE HAZARDOUS TO OUR HEALTH

"Unforgiveness is like drinking poison and expecting the other person to die."
—ANONYMOUS

Having a forgiving heart is the prerequisite to walking in the spiritual freedom that God wants for each of His children. Harboring unforgiveness through offenses and grudges not only blocks the forgiveness we desperately need from God, but is damaging to our physical, mental, and emotional health by opening a door to the enemy.

> "For if you forgive others their trespasses, your heavenly Father will also forgive you, but if you do not forgive others their trespasses, neither will your Father forgive your trespasses" (Mathew 6:14-15, ESV).

> "The human spirit can endure a sick body, but who can bear a crushed spirit?" (Proverbs 18:14, NLT).

> "A joyful, cheerful heart brings healing to both body and soul. But the one whose heart is crushed struggles with sickness and depression" (Proverbs 17:22, TPT).

Walking in daily forgiveness was important to Jesus. This is how He taught us to pray in Matthew 6:9–13, "Our Father in heaven, may your name be kept holy. May your Kingdom come soon. May your will be done on earth, as it is in heaven. Give us today the food we need, and forgive us our sins, as we have forgiven those who sin against us. And don't let us yield to temptation, but rescue us from the evil one" (NLT).

The grace Jesus freely offers to anyone was bought by the most precious of all gifts: His own lifeblood. The *only* thing needed to receive it, is sincere repentance for our sins. The *only* thing needed to keep it, is walking in obedience to His Word. Now it should become apparent why Satan tries so hard to use deception of God's Word to detour us to the crooked road.

"He is the Rock, His work is perfect; For all his ways are justice, A God of truth and without injustice; Righteous and upright is He. They have corrupted themselves; They are not His children, Because of their blemish: A perverse and crooked generation" (Deuteronomy 32:4-5, NKJV).

The crooked road transports those involved in every kind of evil and abomination in God's sight. It also transports many millions who have hardened their heart to God and refuse to receive the greatest gift ever given to humankind. The counterfeit bait the Enemy uses to deceive and ultimately trap us, is alluring. It appears to temporarily meet the need and fill the void we're longing to fill. Sadly, each time it leaves us emptier and desperately wanting more. The difference between what God offers and what Satan offers is as different as day is from night, light is from darkness, good is from evil, and life is from death!

> "And do this, understanding the present time. The hour has come for you to wake up from your slumber, because our salvation is nearer now than when we first believed. The night is nearly over; the day is almost here. So let us put aside the deeds of darkness and put on the armor of light. Let us behave decently, as in the daytime, not in orgies and drunkenness, not in sexual immorality and debauchery, not in dissension and jealousy. Rather, clothe yourselves with the Lord Jesus Christ, and do not think about how to gratify the desires of the sinful nature" (Romans 13:11–14, NIV).

When God created us in His image, He also gave us an extremely powerful gift: the gift of free will. Our Heavenly

Father longs to have a relationship with us, but He refuses to force it! Over and over, the Bible carefully points out that deception destroys. We are responsible for the choices we make in this life and because of this, the place where we will spend eternity literally hangs in the balance.

"Yes, I am the gate. Those who come in through me will be saved. They will come and go freely and will find good pastures. The thief's purpose is to steal and kill and destroy. My purpose is to give them a rich and satisfying life" (John 10:9–10, NLT).

In the absence of God's supernatural presence in our lives, we suffocate with Satan's deceptive counterfeit solutions! Since we rebelliously expelled God from our hearts, our homes, our schools, and our communities—the world is tipping heavily to the side of disastrous separation from God, ultimately bringing total destruction.

WHAT GOD PROVIDES	SATAN'S COUNTERFEIT (AND THE ULTIMATE RESULT)
God (HIMSELF)	Higher Power—(temporal not eternal)
God is LOVE	Attraction—(Lust, promiscuity, pornography, sexual addiction, homosexuality, pedophilia, deviancy)
God is TRUTH	Spirituality—(belief in empty, powerless entities that can't deliver)
God is JOY	Thrill Seeking—(partying, drugs, alcohol, sex, gambling, addiction, adrenaline junkies, death defying stunts)
God is PEACE	Power—(war, anarchy, conflict, greed, chaos, confusion, terrorism)
God is SECURITY	Pride—(insecurity, perfectionism, arrogance, rebellion, narcissism, fear, depression, inferiority, paranoia, suicide)
God is PATIENCE	Control—(impatience, anger, hatred, violence, rage, malice, murder)
God is FREEDOM	License—(slavery, bondage, coerciveness, hopelessness, mental illness, bullying, despondence, human sex trafficking)
God is FORGIVENESS	Self-Reliance—(unforgiveness, grudge holding, offenses, sickness, disease, hatred, torment, death)
God is SABBATH REST	Self-Sufficiency—(exhaustion, restlessness, nervousness, anxiety ridden, over stimulated, over scheduled, agitated, insomnia, highjacked spiritually, physically, mentally, emotionally)

Do you suffer from any of the maladies produced by Satan's deception? If so, thankfully, you now know the first step toward deliverance; **repent** and surrender your life to Jesus, whose blood purchased your salvation, healing, freedom, and deliverance from every bondage and addiction. The price for your deliverance, has already been **PAID IN FULL!**

"BE SOBER-MINDED,

BE ALERT.

YOUR ADVERSARY

THE DEVIL IS PROWLING

AROUND LIKE

A ROARING LION,

LOOKING FOR ANYONE

HE CAN DEVOUR"

—1 PETER 5:8, CSB

DRIVING UNDER THE INFLUENCE

Satan's twisted truth, deceptions, and outright lies can only deceive and conquer us if we allow it. We don't just stumble onto this crooked road, it's a choice. We choose to have a casual relationship with the TRUTH! At every fork and turn in the road we have an opportunity to change our direction, or we can *choose* to keep moving along the same rebellious path. Crooked road travelers like to blame God for every mishap and calamity, when in fact, they're the ones who are choosing to drive under the influence of the great deceiver, Satan. Proverbs 2:12–15 states, "Wisdom will save you from evil people, from those whose words are twisted. These men turn from the right way to walk down dark paths. They take pleasure in doing wrong, and they enjoy the twisted ways of evil. Their actions are crooked, and their ways are wrong" (NLT).

Before we find ourselves on the crooked road of depravity and destruction, we must first choose to ignore the Truth that is readily available to us in the Bible. Second, we must choose to ignore our conscience, that still, small, inner voice that questions our decisions with red flags of doubt and trepidation. Thankfully, because of the blood Jesus willingly shed for our sins, we still have the option of turning back to Him! As long as we have breath in our lungs and sincerely repent of our sins, we *will* be forgiven; unless we wait until it's too late!

I believe a lot of us are living our lives contrary to Scripture. And I believe it's because of the hyper-grace message that it really doesn't matter how we live now; God accepts us just as we are. And there is an element of truth to that, that God does accept us just the way we are. But we're not talking about purity, we're not talking about righteousness from the pulpits, we're not talking about holy living, we're not talking about abstaining from evil in our lives. We've opened up the church doors and embraced everything. And so, the church has filled our corridors and our hallways and our Sanctuaries with a soft Gospel. It's a Gospel of accommodation. We've become more 'seeker sensitive' than we have Holy Spirit sensitive. We don't want to offend anybody, we don't want to deal with the tough issues, we don't want to deal with personal holiness. So therefore, it's very difficult to find in the culture Christian and non-Christian, we just mingle these together.[1]

—TODD WHITE,
Evangelical leader

SPIRITUAL ACCOMMODATION

"If you believe what you like in the gospels,
and reject what you don't like,
it is not the gospel you believe, but yourself."
—ST. AUGUSTINE

It's not surprising that Christianity suffers from severe anemia, when ministers of the gospel in many of the churches today have been cowardly practicing spiritual accommodation to the loudest liberal voices sitting in their pews. Preaching a perverted gospel by diluting and distorting the Word of God, supporting the murdering of the innocent unborn, promoting racial strife and division, contributing to gender dysphoria by rejecting God's divine design of creating one man and one woman, and promoting drag queen celebrations (within the church) which are blasphemous abominations to the gospel message of Jesus Christ and the blood He sacrificially shed on the cross for us! Accepting the title of minister of the gospel of Christ carries with it the holy responsibility of sharing the gospel according to the Word of God.

Tragically, these are some of the greatest offenders traveling the crooked road under the guise of *wolves in sheep's clothing.* What a loving, long-suffering God we serve! It should give us great hope when the Bible is careful to point out the many misguided and malevolent individuals, who rebelled against God with their words or actions, but through sincere repentance were forgiven and their righteousness and divine destiny restored.

SCRIPTURE REFERENCES

If you declare with your mouth, "Jesus is Lord," and believe in your heart that God raised him from the dead, you will be saved (Romans 10:9, NIV).

"I will cleanse them from all the guilt of their sin against me, and I will forgive all the guilt of their sin and rebellion against me" (Jeremiah 33:8, ESV).

"For I will forgive their wickedness, and I will never again remember their sins" (Hebrews 8:12, NLT).

"He has removed our sins as far from us as the east is from the west" (Psalm 103:12, NLT).

"Therefore, if anyone is in Christ, he is a new creation; the old has gone, the new has come!" (2 Corinthians 5:17, NIV).

"BUT IF WE WALK IN THE LIGHT, AS HE IS IN THE LIGHT, WE HAVE FELLOWSHIP WITH ONE ANOTHER, AND THE BLOOD OF JESUS, HIS SON, PURIFIES US FROM ALL SIN".

—1 JOHN 1:7, NIV

REROUTING

In America, enemies of Christ have partnered with spirits of Baal and Jezebel (lust for wealth, power, and perversion), Leviathan (deception and twisting communication), and Witchcraft (mind control), to spin a 3-fold web. Government, education, and media have now trapped our nation in a web of humanism (man is the center, not God), secularism (God removed from all public life), and pluralism (many gods, or ways to God). This unholy trinity is entrenched—its roots are now deep in a generation of brainwashed Americans—and there is no human remedy.[2]

*—*DUTCH SHEETS

We have no *human* remedy . . . but God! God's gifts to us are many and are exceedingly generous and complete! They satisfy in a way that can only be comprehended and experienced through the power of His Holy Spirit. The genuine love, truth, peace, joy, rest, belonging, destiny, and the meaning of life that the world is desperately searching for, are readily available through Jesus Christ and the precious gift of Salvation that His blood purchased for us on the cross. Jesus took our sin and paid the ultimate price to redeem us from the pit of hell. All

He wants in return, is to have a relationship with His Bride (the blood-washed believers in Christ). Your out-of-control life that is barreling down the crooked road towards destruction can easily be rerouted through one name—JESUS!

"Then Jesus said to His disciples, "If anyone wishes to come after Me, he must deny himself, and take up his cross and follow Me. For whoever wishes to save his life will lose it; but whoever loses his life for My sake will find it. For what will it profit a man if he gains the whole world and forfeits his soul? Or what will a man give in exchange for his soul? For the Son of Man is going to come in the glory of His Father with His angels, and will then repay every man according to his deeds" (Matthew 16:24-27, NLT).

THE GRACE JESUS FREELY OFFERS TO ANYONE WAS BOUGHT BY THE MOST PRECIOUS OF ALL GIFTS: HIS OWN LIFEBLOOD.

CHAPTER FOUR:

THE

DIVIDED

ROAD

THE DANGER IN
PLAYING THE MIDDLE
AND FOSTERING
NEUTRALITY IS THAT
IT DIMINISHES GODLY
DISCERNMENT.

4

THE DIVIDED ROAD

"I know your deeds, that you are neither
cold nor hot. I wish you were either one or
the other! So, because you are lukewarm—
neither hot nor cold—I am about to spit
you out of my mouth. You say, 'I am rich;
I have acquired wealth and do not need a
thing.' But you do not realize that you are
wretched, pitiful, poor, blind and naked"
(Revelations 3:15-17, NIV).

Of all the roads we could travel, the divided road is the most soul destroying; for to successfully navigate this road requires continual compromise, leading to moral ambiguity, leading to ultimate godlessness. The divided road is also the most difficult to navigate because of what is required to navigate them. Playing it down the middle or trying to negotiate both sides running in opposite directions, necessitates constant agility and awareness in the best of situations even with full visibility. However, because it is literally impossible to see in both directions at the same time, you are, mostly, traveling blind.

> *"There's nothing commendable about being so impartial between truth and falsity that we split the difference between the two and call it objectivity."*
>
> —PAUL GREENBERG,
> columnist, and author

There are many biblical examples of when the children of God *recognized* demonic spirits. There are also examples of when demonic spirits *recognized* Jesus and His followers. It becomes evident that the two extremes of good and evil are able to recognize that which is diametrically opposed to them. The danger in playing the middle and fostering neutrality is that it diminishes godly discernment. This results in no longer being able to wisely distinguish between good and evil. It's as if you are driving in a heavy fog. One vehicle begins to look like the other and before long you are calling evil good and good evil.

SCRIPTURE REFERENCES

"For that person must not suppose that a double-minded man, unstable in all his ways will receive anything from the Lord" (James 1:7–8, RSV).

"No one can serve two masters, since either he will hate one and love the other, or he will be devoted to one and despise the other. You cannot serve both God and money" (Mathew 6:24, CSB).

"With the tongue we praise our Lord and Father, and with it we curse men, who have been made in God's likeness. Out of the same mouth come praise and cursing. My brothers, this should not be. Can both fresh water and salt water flow from the same spring? My brothers, can a fig tree bear olives, or a grapevine bear figs? Neither can a salt spring produce fresh water" (James 3:9–12, NIV).

"Teach me your way, Lord; that I may rely on your faithfulness; give me an undivided heart, that I may fear your name" (Psalm 86:11, NIV).

God doesn't mince words with how He feels about being double-minded!

> "You adulterous people, don't you know that friendship with the world is hatred toward God? Anyone who chooses to be a friend of the world becomes and enemy of God. Or do you think Scripture says without reason that the spirit he caused to live in us envies intensely? But he gives us more grace. That is why Scripture says: "God opposes the proud but gives grace to the humble. Submit yourselves, then, to God. Resist the devil, and he will flee from you. Come near to God and he will come near to you. Wash your hands, you sinners, and purify your hearts, you double-minded" (James 4:4–10, NIV).

Down through time, cultures and societies have had many names for double mindedness: Speaking with a forked tongue, speaking out of both sides of your mouth, playing both sides against the middle, straddling the fence, taking the middle of the road, walking the yellow line, a best friend to both sides, doesn't take sides, playing both sides of the coin, keeps to the center line, walking the tightrope of popular opinion, telling little white lies, or speaking like a politician. You get the idea.

Doublethink means the power of holding
two contradictory beliefs in one's mind
simultaneously, and accepting both of them.
—GEORGE ORWELL, *1984*

The divided road of double mindedness has led to political correctness. If single-minded *obedience* to Biblical principles results in honesty, integrity, and good character, then *disobedience* to these principles would be the lack thereof. The multitudes that choose the latter group seem to approach critical mass proportions. There are those that wear the label of Christian and yet continue to go along with the anti-biblical, politically correct crowds. For them, the allure of blending in with popular opinion matters more than standing for what is right and pleasing to God. There are also those (leaders, elected officials, celebrities) who say one thing to one group and voice another politically correct opinion elsewhere. Last, there are those who refuse to choose a side by playing it down the middle, which temporarily has its own politically correct reward of plausible deniability. The downside for these unfortunate groups, however, is that God sees the heart!

"Do not love the world nor the things it offers you, for when you love the world, you do not have the love of the Father in you. For the world offers only a craving for physical pleasure, a craving for everything we see, and pride in our achievements and possessions. These are not from the Father, but are from this world. And this world is fading away, along with everything that people crave. But anyone who does what pleases God will live forever" (1 John 2:15–17, NLT).

So much of God's Word, as in the passage above, appears to explode off the page with clarity and a parental protectiveness for His children. We are being reminded that looking, acting, and thinking like the world separates us from the Divine destiny that our loving Heavenly Father has for us. The carnal cravings of the lust of the eyes, the lust of the flesh, and the pride of life are not only short-lived, but also jeopardize our eternal security. Discerning with our spiritual eyes, allows us to see with depth perception that this world is only a temporal vapor, compared to the indescribably beautiful magnificence and perfection of eternity that God has waiting as a reward for each of His children.

THE CANCEL CULTURE
AND WOKENESS

So, we lose our lives by trying to save them,

meaning trying to be accepted by people,

compromising our convictions for our

companions, or becoming a slave to human

opinions. Conversely, we save our lives by

losing them, meaning, by standing for what

is right no matter the cost or consequence.

When we forfeit our lives, in that respect, we

gain our lives. We become free. The cancel

culture can take nothing from us because

we have surrendered our lives to God and

His purposes. In doing so, we die to human

threats. They can no longer hurt us.[3]

—DR. MICHAEL BROWN

No one understands the cancel culture more than Jesus.
For years, His own half-brothers did not fully accept that He
was the Messiah. The powerful priests, elders, and Jews of
His same culture tried to shut Him up for the Truth He was
declaring. The more miracles Jesus performed by healing the
blind, deformed, lame, diseased, demon possessed, and raising

the dead, the more those of His own culture hated Him and tried to kill Him. A sure sign demonic activity is present is that the greater the love and power of Holy Spirit is manifested, the angrier those controlled by Satan become. It was true in Jesus' day, and it is true today.

Wokeness is often referred to as the *propaganda arm of Communism*, for good reason. The deceptive goal of wokeness is slavery of the mind, slavery of the heart, and slavery of the body. Every other thought, opinion, idea, and discourse must be violently quashed. It's been said that if political correctness and a communist bully had a baby, its name would be *Woke*. It goes against our Constitutional rights of free speech and the necessary discourse of public debate (calmly hearing both sides of an issue to rightly discern the truth for ourselves). This deliberate trampling of our first amendment rights is so dangerous, Elon Musk has famously dubbed it the "woke mind virus."

In the not so distant past, when the "Ten Commandments" (see: Are They Ten Commandments or Ten Gifts? *Rabbit Trails Redirect* Vol. 1) were not only displayed in our public schools but regularly recited, there was no question of gray area. Everything was clearly black and white, right and wrong, and good and evil when examined in the light of the ten moral absolutes. Anyone who rebelled against God and the Bible, clearly stood out from the rest, and became the exception. The "Ten Commandments" in the Bible had more influence and direct impact on the lives of the men writing the founding documents of America than any other. This is apparent in the art, sculpture, monument inscriptions, murals, frescos, and paintings in our nation's capital, and the many writings and declarations of our founding fathers. They formed the foundation upon which this nation was built.

DECLINE OF CHRISTIANITY = LIBERAL WISH FULFILLMENT

The persistent God-haters, successful in the removal and moral dismissal of the "Ten Commandments" from schools, courtrooms, and public buildings have precipitated not only a national turning away from Biblical principles but created a growing anathema against Christianity (see: "I'd Become A Christian, If I Hadn't Already Met Some!" *Rabbit Trails Redirect* Vol. 3). This pervasive morality reversal was only possible because many Christians (Bible believing Christ followers) refused to get involved and courageously stand for what they believed in. The pendulum that once swung wide toward obedience to God's Word in the Bible is now rebelliously swinging away from God, His Word, and His people resulting in Christian persecution. This is the epicenter from which the foundation of our nation is beginning to crumble and become dangerously unstable. The first visible crack in our Judeo-Christian foundational beliefs began with the inability to choose a side and take a stand.

We have forgotten God. We have forgotten the gracious hand, which preserved us in peace and multiplied and enriched and strengthened us, and we have vainly imagined, in the deceitfulness of our hearts, that all these blessings were produced by some superior wisdom and virtue of our own. Intoxicated with unbroken success, we have become too self-sufficient to feel the necessity of redeeming and preserving grace, too proud to pray to the God that made us."

—ABRAHAM LINCOLN

This tragedy can't be blamed entirely upon our elected officials, media, and liberal judges. They have been allowed their place of ungodly influence because millions of Christians have abdicated their responsibility by choosing to not take sides or even vote. When it comes time to stand for what they believe, they sit down.

TWO NATURES BEAT
WITHIN MY BREAST

THE ONE IS FOUL,
THE ONE IS BLESSED

THE ONE I LOVE,
THE ONE I HATE,

THE ONE I FEED
WILL DOMINATE.

—ANONYMOUS

When the privilege of voting for those who would have the right to rule over us was at hand, instead of being motivated from a place of deep moral conviction based on Biblical principles and the "Ten Commandments" honoring *all* life (born, preborn, and post born) and God's divine design for family and marriage (one biological man married to one biological woman), many deceptive clergy and deceived Christians continue to vote for whomever the current politically correct crowd clamors after or not at all. When it came to Biblical principles, many CHRINO'S (Christian's In Name Only) stayed silent with their voice and their vote rather than take a stand and make a difference.

The ongoing action of a growing number of government officials and Marxist organizations that ultimately want to eliminate religious freedom will not go away. Religious freedom gets in the way of their utopian goal of governmental control. They don't believe in the United States of America. They don't believe in the Constitution. They only believe in amassing power at your expense. They see the state as the sole authority in all aspects of life. There are many in power at every level of government who see people whose first loyalty is to God as a perpetual threat. They will only be appeased when they can control what you say, think and do. This is why their systematic discrimination and persecution against people of faith will never stop.[4]

—KELLY SHACKELFORD,
First Liberty Institute

IT'S TIME TO STAND YOUR GROUND

"Therefore, put on every piece of God's armor so you will be able to resist the enemy in the time of evil. Then after the battle you will still be standing firm. Stand your ground, putting on the belt of truth and the body armor of God's righteousness" (Ephesians 6:13–14, NLT).

There are those who *claim* to be Christians, and yet vote for politicians who support every policy and choice that are in open rebellion with God and His commandments and principles given to us in His Holy Word such as: abortion, same sex marriage, and the vital interests of Israel. Others choose to vote for whomever would best help their bank accounts. Even worse, some deceived Christians are backing socialist/ Marxist candidates who promise *entitlements and giveaways,* regardless of the candidate's anti-biblical beliefs, their America defeating agenda, or the disastrous assaults on our freedoms these changes will bring.

This sad commentary is reminiscent of many fallen governments of nations past, and casts a revelatory spotlight on the historical truth that most nations that have fallen, have first fallen from *within*. Wisdom and revelation knowledge that can only come from God's Holy Word in the Bible, directs our steps, alerts us to deception, and when we choose to be obedient to God's principles and commandments, also guards us from self-destruction. **Godly wisdom** brings divine clarity of thought, vision, and strength of purpose to first choose God's side, take a stand, and then continue to stand firm in our beliefs, even amid a tidal wave of contrary popular opinion.

"Cowardice asks the question is it safe?
Expediency asks the question, is it politic?
Vanity asks the question, is it popular?
But, conscience asks the question, is it right?
And there comes a time when we
must take a position that is neither
safe, nor politic nor popular, but one
must take it because it is right."
—REV. DR. MARTIN LUTHER KING, JR.

In life, there are many small trials along the way that when passed, strengthen our resolve, and prepare us for the weightier trials. We must pass the small tests of refusing to take part in petty gossip, standing up for someone when they're being made fun of behind their back, or defending a friend or associate when their good character is being insulted or maligned. If we allow someone to cast slanderous aspersions on the integrity of a fellow believer, minister, or ministry, our silence is a form of affirmation ensuring our guilt is the same as those uttering the disparaging words.

However, in the case of "wolves in sheep's clothing," where professing believers and/or ministers in Christ are openly defaming or denying the basic tenets of the Bible, we are called to practice the Matthew 18 principle. Matthew 18:15–17 instructs us about how to handle this situation. "If another believer sins against you, go privately, and point out the offense. If the other person listens and confesses it, you have won that person back. But if you are unsuccessful, take one or two others with you and go back again, so that everything you say may be confirmed by two or three witnesses. If the person still refuses to listen, take your case to the church. Then if he or she won't accept the church's decision, treat that person as a pagan or a corrupt tax collector" (NLT).

SCRIPTURE REFERENCES

"Fear of man will prove to be a snare, but whoever trusts in the Lord is kept safe" (Proverbs 29:25, NIV).

"Everyone who acknowledges me publicly here on earth, I will also acknowledge before my Father in heaven" (Mathew 10:32, NLT).

"If anyone is ashamed of me and my message in these adulterous and sinful days, the Son of Man will be ashamed of that person when he returns in the glory of his Father with the holy angels" (Mark 8:38, NLT).

If we refuse to take a stand for Truth in the small tests, how will we ever be trusted to do the right thing in the big ones? Yes, it's hard to lovingly take a stand against the razor-tongued crowd that is immersed in the anti-biblical religion of political correctness, yet, not taking a stand for Truth counts us among their number.

Truth will ultimately prevail

where there is pains to bring it to light.

— GEORGE WASHINGTON,
First U.S. President

Simply standing for God and His eternal principles amid our daily activities, both within our circle of influence and those who cross our path, may well be the single most important task put before us in our lifetime. No one looks forward to ridicule, much less when it's in a public setting, and it's certainly not pleasant sticking out like a sore thumb amid those who could easily turn and rail against us. There comes a time in everyone's life where an eternal choice needs to be made: to be conformed to this world, or be transformed by the renewing of your mind through the Truth of God's Word!

STANDING IN THE MIDDLE OF THE ROAD IS DANGEROUS. YOU WILL GET KNOCKED DOWN BY THE TRAFFIC FROM BOTH WAYS.

— MARGARET THATCHER,
FORMER BRITISH PRIME MINISTER

We might think we can get away with merely going through life without making a choice or taking sides, but tragically, choosing to *not* make a choice *is* making a choice. Out of God's merciful love, the coming catastrophic end-time events will ensure that everyone will ultimately *have* to make a choice. Will we choose the easy way by taking the side of the crowd championing carnal, temporal reasoning, or the side of TRUTH which counts for eternity?

If some among you fear taking a stand
because you are afraid of reprisals from
customers, clients, or even government,
recognize that you are just feeding
the crocodile hoping he'll eat you last.
—RONALD REAGAN,
U.S. President

What will it take for us to learn from our mistakes? Playing the middle is a dangerous game and our *fear of man* can ultimately lead to bondage, destruction, and even death. Too many are negotiating the divided road and have become blinded to the evil and deception all around them and will see the fulfillment of the old adage, "If you don't learn from the mistakes of the past, you're destined to repeat them!"

2 Corinthians 11:3 reads, "But I fear, lest somehow, as the serpent deceived Eve by his craftiness, so your minds may be corrupted from the simplicity that is in Christ" (KJV).

> *In 2 Corinthians 11:3 simplicity is the Greek word haplotes. Its most literal meaning is "singleness, without dissimulation or duplicity," (3) or "the opposite of duplicity." (4) The verse is saying that, in our devotion to Christ, we must not be double-minded. We must guard against anything causing dissimulation, division, or a watering down. It is okay to be multifaceted in our gifts and activity, and it is wise to be broad-based in our understanding, but in our approach to relationship with Jesus we must be very single-minded. Allow no other person or activity to crowd Him out. To take Him for granted or allow Him to simply be one of many priorities will weaken us.*[5]
>
> —DUTCH SHEETS

James 1:7–8 tells us all it takes to change from being this person,

"That man should not think he will receive anything from the Lord; he is a double-minded man, unstable in all he does" (NIV).

To being this person:

"Teach me your way, O Lord, and I will walk in your truth; give me an undivided heart, that I may fear your name" (Psalm 86:11, NIV).

It only takes a changed heart—which is God's specialty!

"Create in me a clean heart, O God, and renew a right spirit within me" (Psalm 51:10, ESV).

THE FIRST VISIBLE CRACK IN OUR JUDEO-CHRISTIAN FOUNDATIONAL BELIEFS BEGAN WITH THE INABILITY TO CHOOSE A SIDE AND TAKE A STAND.

CHAPTER FIVE:

THE

OPEN

ROAD

WHEN WE CHOOSE TO
ABDICATE OUR GOD-GIVEN
FREEWILL TO SEARCH
FOR TRUTH ON OUR
OWN, WE'RE MAKING THE
CHOICE TO SETTLE FOR
THE TEMPORAL RATHER
THAN THE ETERNAL. WE
OPT FOR DRIVEL, RATHER
THAN THE DIVINE.

5

THE OPEN ROAD

"I urge you, brothers, to watch out for those
who cause divisions and put obstacles
in your way that are contrary to the teaching
you have learned. Keep away from them.
For such people are not serving our Lord Christ,
but their own appetites. By smooth talk and
flattery they deceive the minds of naive people"
(Romans 16:17–18, NIV).

In America we are blessed to live in a free society where an *open* tolerance of every religion and belief system is not only accepted but encouraged. This is exactly what freedom is all about! However, the smorgasbord of religious choices can be confusing, especially with the deeper questions of life. After all, with the plethora of diverse and often contradictory ways and means to navigate life's journey from beginning to end and then to the hereafter, how can they all be right?

Although the Bible clearly teaches the only way to eternal salvation is through Jesus Christ, many individuals and even ministers of the gospel and their churches seem to ignore this, as they travel down the open road of rebellion against God. The blessings of salvation, forgiveness, healing, deliverance, unity, and love for our neighbor (regardless of race or skin color) miraculously overflow from our heart when the truth of the gospel of Jesus Christ is righteously preached from the pulpit.

Tragically, the sacrificial blood of Jesus that forgives our sins, heals our diseases, and delivers us from bondages and addictions—has been replaced with abortion rights, transgenderism, race hustlers, victim hustlers, hate hustlers, and anything goes (as long as it's politically correct and promotes the liberal agenda). For obvious reasons, the high speed and extremely popular open road of life is the widest, most deceptive, most congested, and ultimately the most destructive of all the roads.

This open "all inclusive" mega highway mode of transportation is heading straight for a cliff. If you saw someone heading for a cliff, wouldn't you want to warn them? Many of us have heard the words piously repeated, "All roads lead to God, whatever road you choose will get you there." The most common rebuttals to living a biblically obedient lifestyle are: "It's my life, don't tell me what to do," or "This is my reality and I'm choosing to live my reality," and their favorite, "How could Christianity be so arrogant as to say the only way to heaven is through Jesus?"

> You have come to Jesus, the one who medi-
> ates the new covenant between God and
> people, and to the sprinkled blood, which
> speaks of forgiveness instead of crying
> out for vengeance like the blood of Abel.
> (Hebrews 12:24 NLT)

The open road is congested with those speeding away from the "Absolutes" in the Bible, but absolutes are God's idea. John 14:6 tells us, "Jesus answered, 'I am the way and the truth and the life. No one comes to the Father except through me'" (NIV). God's absolutes not only give us warning signs to avoid danger but prevent us from going over the cliff—if they're obeyed.

GOD'S ABSOLUTES IN THE BIBLE

GOD	SATAN
Good	evil
Light	darkness
Love	hate
Truth	lies
Peace	anarchy
Savior	deceiver
Freedom	slavery
Creator	destroyer
Order	chaos
Faith	fear
Joy	sorrow
Intimacy	rejection
Security	abandonment
Fellowship	isolation
Worship	rebellion
Life	death
Heaven	Hell

SELF-EVIDENT TRUTH

If you pay attention to God's Word in the Bible, He lovingly demonstrates the clear-cut choices we've been given, to carefully warn us away from deception and the many snares of Satan.

> "The thief comes only to steal and kill and destroy. I came that they may have life and have it abundantly" (John 10:10, ESV).

A deep chasm lies between the fruits of God and the fruits of Satan. There will never be a point of proximity, comparison, or similarity between God and Satan, as Satan would have us to believe. Satan flaunts the deception that sympathy, empathy, tolerance, and compassion *for sin* casually resides in an imaginary gray area between him and God. Our loving, compassionate, and long-suffering Heavenly Father only asks one thing from His beloved children—for us to make a choice.

The absolutes of creation are not rocket science. Many defiant and deluded minds who are steeped in rebellion that has taken root in their hearts, insist there are no moral absolutes, but even a small child can see the difference between good and evil, light and darkness, truth and lies.

THE MOMENT OF TRUTH

Which category does the fruit from your life fall under? Acknowledging the existence of these absolutes, recognizing the source for both, and choosing God's side is the first step of wisdom toward truth and freedom. The magnificence of creation undeniably having an intelligent divine designer is self-evident to all and can intimately be perceived by the pure in heart who are open to God's Truth. Romans 1:18–20 confirms this truth, "The wrath of God is being revealed from heaven against all the godlessness and wickedness of people, who suppress the truth by their wickedness, since what may be known about God is plain to them, because God has made it plain to them. For since the creation of the world God's invisible qualities—his eternal power and divine nature—have been clearly seen, being understood from what has been made, so that people are without excuse" (NIV).

THE OPEN ROAD OF FALSE NARRATIVE

The open road of laziness, license (control), and lasciviousness was birthed in Satan's desire to hijack God's loving plan of redemption for His children. Satan plants his disarmingly false narrative as close to God's Holy Truth as possible. He starts with religious pluralism, the deceptive philosophy that all religions and cults will basically lead you to the same destination, and moves on to Agnosticism, the uncertainty of whether God actually exists (cutting His Son Jesus Christ our sinless Savior out of the picture), and then finally to Atheism, the belief that there is no God (canceling God our Father, Jesus and His priceless blood sacrifice for us, and Holy Spirit who leads and empowers us). The cancel culture is not a new thing. The current woke culture is merely taking their cues from their father Satan, the originator of attempting to cancel *everything that is of God,* which is ultimately what the cancel culture is all about, but the Bible tells us they will ultimately FAIL!

Satan, the prince of darkness, masquerades as an angel of light and his followers will do exactly the same. They religiously pretend to come in peace with the weighted dialogue of tolerance and openness, while cleverly disguising the burning cauldron of hatred in their heart that has blackened their souls against Christians and Jews. They pretend to champion children, the poor, the under-privileged, homeless, and help-less, while barbarically fighting for the right to murder the *most* helpless of all, the innocent unborn, and now newborn, human babies. They pretend to be open-minded and tolerant of every belief, philosophy, religion, lifestyle, and woke agenda; except toward the believers in Christ who obediently stand for biblical principles—of whom they are openly hostile.

> "These people are false apostles. They are deceitful workers who disguise themselves as apostles of Christ. But I am not surprised! Even Satan disguises himself as an angel of light. So it is no wonder that his servants also disguise themselves as servants of righteousness. In the end they will get the punishment their wicked deeds deserve" (2 Corinthians 11:13-15, NLT).

The Bible warns us not only of false religions, but more specifically of false apostles, prophets, ministers, priests, and teachers who appear as wolves in sheep's' clothing. They espouse peace, openness, light, love, tolerance, and acceptance of every belief or lifestyle of sin, without *first* pointing people toward Jesus Christ for salvation and healing. Mathew 7:15 reads, "Be on your guard against false prophets who come to you in sheep's clothing but inwardly are ravaging wolves. You'll recognize them by their fruit" (CSB).

We also have politicians and even past Presidents who have claimed to be a Christian, but the fruit of their anti-biblical decisions and America destroying agenda proved to be the exact opposite, revealing we'd been lied to, once again. Jesus Christ mercifully loved the sinner but hated the sin. He sees our hearts and knows who is genuine and who is pretending. We have this assurance, along with those in the Bible who were steeped in sin and yet repented; Jesus loved, healed, and forgave them and then said, "Go and sin no more."

JESUS = LOVE BALANCED WITH TRUTH

Jesus is our perfect example of love equally balanced with truth. Christ's love without biblical truth, or biblical truth without Christ's love, are blasphemous misrepresentations of the redemptive gospel message of grace, truth, and forgiveness that Jesus was excruciatingly tortured, bled, died, and rose again to bring to you and me. "For from his fullness we have all received, grace upon grace. For the law was given through Moses; grace and truth came through Jesus Christ" (John 1:16–17, BSB).

Satan's main mission is to "steal, kill and destroy," as the Bible warns. What we are missing is the blatant, open deception right under our noses in the church. It's easy for Satan to fool the foolish, mislead the misled, and defeat the already defeated. His most heinous deceptions, however, occur within anti-biblical religions, anti-biblical denominations, and Christianity itself, when the gospel message of Christ is diluted and distorted. When we don't know what the Word of God says for ourselves, we are *asking* to be deceived.

Jesus' life on earth was given to us not only for our salvation, healing, deliverance, and eternal security, but as our perfect example to follow. His life was balanced. If we had to summarize the example Jesus left for us, it would be **Love** balanced with **Truth/Justice**.

Jesus called out and confronted the religious extremes, the ultra-religious, legalistic Pharisees who were blinded to the Truth of God's Love because they couldn't see past the Law. On the other extreme were those believing that the New Covenant of grace they received through the cross of Christ afforded them free license to go on sinning. Legalism and the hyper-Grace emergent church movement are still around deceiving and corrupting today (see: "Are They Ten Commandments or Ten Gifts, 'Third Commandment' *Rabbit*

Trails Redirect Vol. 1). Romans 10:4 tells us, "For Christ has already accomplished the purpose for which the law was given. As a result, all who believe in him are made right with God" (NLT).

OUR DESTINY IS FOUND BETWEEN GOD'S LOVE AND JUSTICE

Even though God loves us with a LOVE so superior that our minds can't fully comprehend it, He is also a God of Justice (see: "How Can A Good God Let Bad Things Happen?" *Rabbit Trails Redirect*). These attributes of God's character are not mutually exclusive but divinely balanced to fulfill His promises to those who are obedient to His Word. Our heavenly Father longs to bless His obedient children, and His Word lovingly warns that the deceptive open road of license, lust, and laziness leads us *away* from His blessing.

> "And this is love: that we walk in obedience
> to his commands. As you have heard from
> the beginning, his command is that you walk
> in love" (2 John 1:6, NIV).

God's Word brings light to the darkness, and o*bedience* to God's Word is the key. Obedience to someone else's words, no matter how high their global religious position, prominence, and power might be, leads to death. Someone else's version of truth through a dream, angelic visitation, manifestation, hallucination, or drunken grandiose envisioning does not lead to eternal life. Some self-anointed guru, cult figure, or Christ-impersonator's dilution or distortion of the truth are not the way to salvation. And murderous laws passed by our government that allow the child-sacrifice and murder of help-less unborn human babies again leads to death and destruction. In God's eyes, a "man-decreed law" doesn't make it moral or acceptable. (see: "Women's Choices-The Right to Murder" *Rabbit Trails Redirect*). Only obedience to the **truth** of God's Holy, inerrant Word will direct our steps on the path toward our divine destiny. We must finally acknowledge that distance from His Light *welcomes* darkness and distance from His Word *invites* deception.

We desperately long to find the answers to our questions without having to give up any of our self-proclaimed *rights*. We diligently search the open road to find the truth that doesn't require us to change our way of thinking or living. How determinedly we grapple with the incessant need to define the undefinable, to explain the unexplainable, prove the unprovable; in other words, we pridefully attempt to put God, the Creator of the Universe, in a box.

> "God opposes the proud but gives grace to the humble. Humble yourselves, therefore, under God's mighty hand, that he may lift you up in due time. Cast all your anxiety on him because he cares for you" (1 Peter 5:5–6, NIV).

The open road leads to many avenues of enticing, yet dead-end spirituality. We embrace the non-threatening, cuddly blankets of *spiritual fluff in order to feel good.* We swallow something deliciously palatable that does not convict us in our spirit, hold us accountable to a divine standard, conflict with our choices, or require us to take a courageous stand of **faith**. The initial spoonful of deliciousness quickly dissipates leaving us with the empty, unsatisfied craving we had before. The only way that our soul will ever be truly satisfied, and our divine destiny discovered is when we choose to surrender complete control to Jesus as our Lord and Savior.

God's love and justice stand like mighty signposts on each side of His narrow road, directing us to our divine destiny. He promises that "You will seek me and find me; when you seek me with all your heart." During this time of societal and social unrest, many hurting and hungry souls are crying out for social justice but refuse to leave the open road of political correctness and convenience for the less convenient way. There is only One who can deliver genuine truth and justice and His Name is Jesus—the Way, the Truth, and the Life. The prideful and powerful global "elite" (as they like to call themselves) despise and consider foolish those who choose the narrow road.

> "Remember, dear brothers and sisters, that few of you were wise in the world's eyes or powerful or wealthy when God called you. Instead, God chose things the world considers foolish in order to shame those who think they are wise. And he chose things that are powerless to shame those who are powerful. God chose things despised by the world, things counted as nothing at all, and used them to bring to nothing what the world considers important. As a result, no one can ever boast in the presence of God" (1 Corinthians 1:26-30, NLT).

There are no neon signs or flood lights splashing the sky

to direct us to the subtle and unadorned narrow road and yet the generous and easily accessible wisdom and light emanating from God's Word directs our path to the beautiful destiny for which we were created.

RELATIONSHIP IS PERSONAL, NOT BORROWED

"Trust in the Lord with all your heart, And lean not on your own understanding; In all your ways acknowledge him, And He shall direct your paths" (Proverbs 3:5-6, NKJV).

Many people are being deceived by traveling down this open road of feel-good, dessert spirituality. Perhaps it's easier to blindly embrace *another's'* belief system because of their celebrity, wealth, or public prominence, rather than carefully investing in our own biblical due diligence. It could be many things including laziness, defiance, rebellion, idolatry, or deception that causes us to turn to others for our answers instead of to God. The Bible warns about being led astray by false doctrines and the worship of idols. So much so that God made it #2 on His list of commandments (see: "Are They Ten Commandments or Ten Gifts?" *Rabbit Trails Redirect* Vol. 1).

Knowledge is a good thing! The Bible tells us that "we perish for lack of knowledge." It also prophetically tells us that in the last days knowledge will increase rapidly. We are witnessing this information explosion all around us. We operate numerous "Apps" while navigating multiple media sites which are available on all of our personal devices (computers, phones, tablets, rings, watches, and immensely anticipated eyeglasses). Virtually limitless information can now be accessed with our voice or fingertips within seconds.

Depending on our choices, the internet consumption can either be used to expand our knowledge on a particular subject or be a time-wasting, soul-destroying distraction. Unfortunately, because of this convenient access to useless information, many have become disturbingly engrossed and even idolatrously addicted to following the daily activities of celebrity worship. Apart from a genuine relationship with Jesus who supernaturally satisfies all of our longings, we will attempt to grasp at anything to momentarily fill the cavernous void within us.

Whether its celebrities made famous by big tech, sports, politics, movies, television, modeling, or reality shows, we've allowed ourselves to become continually bombarded by constant updates from Tweets, YouTube videos, Instagram and others. These continuous updates highlight their enviable fame, power, lifestyles, stratospheric income, world travel, designer apparel, and don't forget their houses, cars, planes, and jewelry. With the carnal void within us longing to be filled, we allow this mindless entertainment and escapism to temporarily satiate our need. Anything that comes before or takes the place of God the Father, Son, and Holy Spirit in our lives, can become an idol and worshiped. In Exodus 20:3 God said, "You shall have no other gods before Me" (NKJV). And in Isaiah 42:8 He declared, "I am the Lord! That is my name! I will not share my glory with anyone else, or the praise due me with idols" (NET).

Idol worship can unfortunately include godly clergy, Mary, the mother of Jesus, saints of the Bible, religiously declared saints of this world, the Pope, and even other ministries' social media sites (blogs, tweets, Instagram, podcasts) that we allow to circumvent or detour our time spent in intimate fellowship with our Heavenly Father and in His Word. God desires to have a personal relationship with *us*, not us through someone else. Satan's open road of smoke and mirrors is designed to throw up smoke screens *in every direction* to prevent us from the intimate relationship with our Savior that we were created to enjoy!

The Bible reminds us we are to be "wise as serpents and harmless as doves." When our eyes *choose* to turn away from obedience to God and His Holy Word, the God-*less* void easily becomes filled with spiritual imposters.

> "Behold, I send you out as sheep in the midst
> of wolves. Therefore be wise as serpents and
> harmless as doves" (Matthew 10:16, NKJV).

Traveling the mindless open road of popular opinion leads to accepting someone else's beliefs, religion, politically correct philosophy or blasphemous new and improved distortion of Christianity, such as in Synchronism, which mixes 2 or more religions together (example: Chrislam or Christian Agnostics). Not searching for the Truth on our own, which can only be found in the Bible, is like copying down the answers to a test from someone else's paper. We risk failure and may forfeit our eternal reward, as well.

When it comes to eternity, we either pass or fail the test *by choice*. When we choose to abdicate our God-given freewill to search for truth on our own, we're making the choice to settle for the temporal rather than the eternal. We opt for drivel, rather than the divine. Tragically, many blindly follow

another person's path and choices because of their fame, fortune, celebrity, or notoriety.

> *"It gives me a moral compass, I often refer*
> *to Abe Lincoln, who said, "When I do good,*
> *I feel good. When I do bad, I feel bad."*
> *And that is my religion. I think we all have*
> *a little voice inside us that will guide us. It*
> *may be God, I don't know. But I think that*
> *if we shut out all the noise and clutter from*
> *our lives and listen to that voice, it will*
> *tell us the right thing to do. The Unitarian*
> *believes that God is good, and believes that*
> *God believes that man is good. Inherently.*
> *The Unitarian God is not a God of vengeance.*
> *And that is something I can appreciate."* [6]
>
> —CHRISTOPHER REEVE,
> actor

Many anti-biblical beliefs have an accommodatingly peaceful and comforting tone, yet deceptively **defy** what the Bible teaches. Unfortunately, there are those going through life with a completely wrong mindset of who God really is. He is a good Father and a God of Love (the very *Source of Love*), balanced with Truth and Justice. As any *good* father parents his child, our loving heavenly Father not only gives us rules to follow for our best interest but also holds us accountable for our obedience to them. Ask anyone in law enforcement how quickly society unravels when you have laws that are not enforced? Listening to the deceptive voice of "self" that often lies to us, rather than the voice of God our Savior who speaks to us from His Holy Word, is a recipe for disaster!

SCRIPTURE REFERENCES

"For God presented Jesus as the sacrifice for sin. People are made right with God when they believe that Jesus sacrificed his life, shedding his blood. This sacrifice shows that God was being fair when he held back and did not punish those who sinned in times past, for he was looking ahead and including them in what he would do in this present time. God did this to demonstrate his righteousness, for he himself is fair and just, and he declares sinners to be right in his sight when they believe in Jesus" (Romans 3:25–26, NLT).

"For I was born a sinner—yes, from the moment my mother conceived me. But you desire honesty from the womb, teaching me wisdom even there. Purify me from my sins, and I will be clean; wash me, and I will be whiter than snow" (Psalm 51:5–7, NLT).

DETOURS FROM JUSTICE

In the Bible, Romans 3 teaches us God is both loving and just. He is our perfect example of a good parent, rewarding obedience and disciplining disobedience. God's biblical example of holding evil in check by punishing evildoers is His divine blueprint for a peaceful, civil, and balanced society. This plan for peace is categorically rejected by those traveling the open road of moral relativism, secular humanism, liberalism, nihilism, Agnosticism, Socialism, Communism, Atheism, Fascism, Globalism, and all the other *isms* that Satan conjures up. "Righteousness and justice are the foundation of your throne; steadfast love and faithfulness go before you" (Psalms 89:14, ESV).

Societal chaos is sure to erupt when this divine balance is disrupted. Wisdom dictates that in any area of life it is imperative that the laws of business, finance, education, commerce, government, law enforcement, and national defense be balanced with justice. God is the origin of justice. As we are now witnessing not only in our nation, but worldwide, detours away from God result in departures from justice. The consequences for both the willful breaking of our laws and justice being withheld or denied, is producing chaos reeling wildly out of control from both sides of the unbalanced scales.

THE OPEN ROAD TO ANARCHY AND GODLESSNESS

Even to the biblically unaware and uninformed, the undeniable stench of anarchy is beginning to be detected in many different areas of society. The absolutes in the Bible clearly show us that the source of anarchy is Satan. We question why any sane person or group of people would deliberately tear at the fabric of our country, thread by thread, with the goal of unraveling our Constitution, weakening our nation, and ultimately destroying it.

The radically liberal, Socialist/Communist, anti-God, anti-Bible, anti-America, anti-Constitution, anti-military, and law-breaking globalists rabidly HATE the God-loving, Bible-believing, law-abiding, Constitution loving, military supporting, America-loving conservatives. Why? Because the America-strengthening, *believers in Christ* have stood in the way of the God-hating globalists' evil agenda of world domination (one-world everything)[7] World Health Organization, World Economic Forum, World Trade Organization, World Bank, World Intellectual Property Organization, World/International Court of Justice.

For the globalist agenda to be achieved; America, the once strong "Superpower" who openly trusted in God (in our pledge and on our money) must be brought down![8] This is accomplished through the globalist-controlled and subsidized (traitors) they have stealthily placed in local, state, and federal positions of government, media, big tech, judiciary, education, and what we're finding to be unexpectedly lethal, big pharma. The initial idea or "domino technique" for destroying America worked just as they had planned, first through pandemic shutdowns and lockdowns that bankrupted businesses, factories, and agriculture. Livestock, poultry, and dairy producers, along with fresh produce growers were forced to destroy multiple millions of inventories of chickens, pigs, milk, and perishable fruits and vegetables that would normally be consumed by schools and restaurants who were forced to remain closed.[9]

Second, this *deliberately* created an opportunity for the government to start sending "Covid stimulus checks," thereby creating a worker shortage, because many of the workers in industrial factories, restaurants, and retail made more money by collecting the checks and staying home. Third, for many, it also fostered a greater dependance on the government as their savior.

The inevitable shipping and supply line blockages and shortages that crippled businesses and industries would have crashed our economy, except for the Central banking system (controlled by the globalists) ability to print more money, causing sky-high inflation.[10] The globalist-controlled "acting" President reversed America's vibrant energy independence on his first day in office, by blocking production and new oil leases, shutting down a vital pipeline, and forcing America to pay higher energy costs from an unfriendly nation.

Next, the globalists' plan for America involves food scarcity and famine. Agricultural whistleblowers have been coming forward (before, during, and even after the shutdown) showing generous government checks they've received for destroying their fully planted and in many cases *ready to harvest* fields. Hundreds of thousands of acres, possibly millions, have been destroyed at the government's behest by plowing under or setting fire to these precious commodities. Food shortages have also now become evident due to "unknown" arsonists deliberately destroying over 70 food distribution plants across our nation, while the complicit mainstream media is *suspiciously silent*. We are completely blinded to the fact we are at war!

America has been deliberately attacked from within, putting our hard-won Constitutional freedoms and everything we hold dear in jeopardy. After obviously fraudulent elections and a subsequent Socialist/Communist takeover, our strong energy-independent America has experienced a multi-industry treasonous assault and reduced to a nation in serious decline in a matter of months. If you want to know what plans they have for America, look to the once beautiful, prosperous, and thriving nations of Cuba and Venezuela. Better yet, ask the people of these gutted nations how they enjoy their food shortages, substandard medical care, and complete loss of freedom?

To pull off the "heist of the century," as any James Bond screenwriter will tell you, first you create a diversion. How do the globalists divert attention away from the Communist takeover of our country? How do you cover your tracks when the economy is tanking, gas prices are soaring, inflation is the highest it's been since the Great Depression, grocery shelves are becoming bare, and looting and rioting in the streets are soon to follow? Start a war and blame everything on the war! Conservatives, but primarily Christian conservatives, who walk in obedience to biblical principles (filling the believer with divine wisdom), are the last line of defense, preventing the Satan-inspired globalist plan of deliberately crippling America, by making it too weak to resist a Communist takeover.[11]

The Bible tells us that in the last days, those who are not walking in God's divine wisdom, power, and authority, which comes through His Word and the anointing of His Holy Spirit, *will be deceived*, most likely by the smooth-tongued, God-hating governmental leaders and corrupted media. Unfortunately, as a result many will believe their lies, follow their destructive agenda, and then stand in line holding out their hands (or arm) for more! The deceived cannot see what is happening right before their eyes because they are *blinded* by deception.

SCRIPTURE REFERENCES

"Your leaders are rebels, the companions of thieves. All of them love bribes and demand payoffs, but they refuse to defend the cause of orphans or fight for the rights of widows" (Isaiah 1:23, NLT).

"Their words are unreliable. Destruction is in their hearts, drawing people into their darkness with their speeches. They are smooth-tongued deceivers, flattering with their words. Declare them guilty, O God! Let their own schemes be their downfall! Let the guilt of their sins collapse on top of them, for they rebel against you" (Psalms 5:9–10, TPT).

"Then he said, "You son of the devil, full of every sort of deceit and fraud, and enemy of all that is good! Will you never stop perverting the true ways of the Lord? (Acts 13:10, NLT).

"They are senseless, faithless, ruthless, heartless, and completely merciless. Although they are fully aware of God's laws and proper order, and knowing that those who do all of these things deserve to die, yet they still go headlong into darkness, encouraging others to do the same and applauding them when they do! (Romans 1:31–32, TPT).

Leading Virologists and Epidemiologists around the world spoke up about the questionable origins of the Covid-19 virus, showing verifiable microscopic evidence of it having been manipulated to become more lethal and not naturally occurring. This dire revelation along with scientists who revealed the vaccine lot #'s showing varying strengths of what were ultimately lethal doses of vaccine being shipped to certain locations/states further exposes the globalists sinister plot![12,13,14] Those that bravely spoke up and revealed this virus as being manipulated in a lab *for evil intentions* were immediately de-platformed (canceled and silenced), their highly esteemed medical credentials besmirched, both they and their family's lives threatened, and were quickly labeled as conspiracy theorists. Thankfully, time has proven these courageous world-renowned scientists correct in their assessment that this pandemic was in reality, a globalist "plan-demic." [15] Deuteronomy 31:6 tells us, "Be strong and of good courage, do not fear nor be afraid of them; for the Lord your God, He is the One who goes with you. He will not leave you nor forsake you" (NKJV).

END-TIMES OPEN EVIL HAS BEEN UNLEASHED

(Globalist depopulation agenda through abortion, sterilization, and vaccines)

"But know this, that in the last days peril-ous times will come: For men will be lovers of themselves, lovers of money, boasters, proud, blasphemers, disobedient to parents, unthankful, unholy, unloving, unforgiving, slanderers, without self-control, brutal, despisers of good, traitors, head-strong, haughty, lovers of pleasure rather than lovers of God, having a form of godliness but deny-ing its power. And from such people turn away! (2 Timothy 3:1-5, NKJV).

First, we've got population. The world today

has 6.8 billion people. That's headed up to

about nine billion. Now, if we do a really

great job on new vaccines, health care,

reproductive health services, we could lower

that by, perhaps, 10 or 15 percent.[16,17]

—BILL GATES, eugenicist, billionaire
philanthropist, TED Talk 2010

We're all 5 billion of us on this little earth

swimming around in space, and there's too many of us.

A total (world) population of 250-300 million people,

a 95% decline from present levels, would be ideal.

—TED TURNER, billionaire philanthropist,
1996 Audubon magazine quote

ALL OF OUR PROBLEMS ARE
THE RESULT OF OVERBREEDING
AMONG THE WORKING CLASS.[18,19]

—MARGARET SANGER,

EUGENICIST, PLANNED PARENTHOOD FOUNDER

In the event that I am reincarnated,

I would like to return as a deadly

virus, in order to contribute something

to solve over-population.[20]

—PRINCE PHILIP, DUKE OF EDINBURGH,
Husband of Queen Elizabeth II

WE NEED TO CONTINUE TO DECREASE THE GROWTH RATE OF THE GLOBAL POPULATION; THE PLANET CAN'T SUPPORT MANY MORE PEOPLE. [21]

—NINA FEDOROFF,
KEY ADVISER TO HILLARY CLINTON

You cannot sleep well when you think it's all

paid by the government. This won't be solved

unless you let them hurry up and die. (regarding

medical patients with serious illnesses).[22]

—TARO ASO,
Japan's Deputy Prime Minister

A program of sterilizing women after their second or third child, despite the relatively greater difficulty of the operation than vasectomy, might be easier to implement than trying to sterilize men. The development of a long-term sterilizing capsule that could be implanted under the skin and removed when pregnancy is desired opens additional possibilities for coercive fertility control. The capsule could be implanted at puberty and might be removable with official permission, for a limited number of births.[23]

—JOHN P. HOLDREN,
Barack Obama's primary science advisor

The most merciful thing that the large family does to one of its infant members is to kill it.[24, 25]

—MARGARET SANGER,
Founder of Planned Parenthood

If there were a button I could press, I would sacrifice myself without hesitating if it meant millions of people would die. [26]

—PENTTI LINKOLA,
Finnish environmentalist

In order to stabilize world population, we must eliminate 350,000 people per day. It is a horrible thing to say, but it is just as bad not to say it.[27]

—JACQUES COSTEAU

CHILDBEARING [SHOULD BE] A PUNISHABLE CRIME AGAINST SOCIETY, UNLESS THE PARENTS HOLD A GOVERNMENT LICENSE… ALL POTENTIAL PARENTS [SHOULD BE] REQUIRED TO USE CONTRACEPTIVE CHEMICALS, THE GOVERNMENT ISSUING ANTIDOTES TO CITIZENS CHOSEN FOR CHILDBEARING.[28]

—DAVID BROWER,
THE FIRST EXECUTIVE DIRECTOR OF THE SIERRA CLUB

We must speak more clearly about sexuality,
contraception, about abortion, about values
that control population, because the ecological
crisis, in short, is the population crisis.
Cut the population by 90% and there aren't enough
left to do a great deal of ecological damage.
—MIKHAIL GORBACHEV

Frankly I had thought that at the time Roe was
decided, there was concern about population
growth and particularly growth in populations
that we don't want to have too many of.[29]
—RUTH BADER GINSBURG,
U.S. Supreme Court Justice

eugenics: the practice or advocacy of
controlled selective breeding of human
populations (as by sterilization) to improve
the population's genetic composition.
—MARIAM-WEBSTER DICTIONARY[30, 31]

depopulate: 1. to remove or reduce the
population of: cities depopulated by plagues.
—WORD REFERENCE
(online language dictionaries)

This is not a secret! The globalists have been expressing their desires to depopulate the earth for decades and have openly declared their timeline of completion by 2030.[32] Klaus Schwab has stated that everyone in the world will be chipped by 2026.[33] I would like to believe this is wishful thinking on their part; however, in lieu of the simultaneously orchestrated, globally catastrophic events and power grab that has already killed millions in two years (even though the corrupt media is not reporting this), many are awakening to the realization that this powerful and centralized control of the world, is in fact, the end-times prophetic scripture of an Antichrist controlled one-world government beginning to be fulfilled.

As if the Satan-inspired globalists planning the world-wide plague(s) to ensure the depopulation of billions wasn't enough, by following the "gain of function" money-trail[34], evidence has uncovered that not only was our government, along with billionaire globalists, doctors, and scientists (some of whom were enlisted as trusted spokespersons throughout the entire "plandemic") complicit in the evil "gain of function" debacle, but were heavily financially invested and remunerated by the corrupt big Pharma, as well, and stood to gain millions *by prolonging the suffering to create vaccine demand.*[35,36,37]

This is the classic "asking the fox to guard the henhouse." Not only did the globalist THUGS create vaccine demand by their continual and prolonged fear mongering through the media, but they grossly exaggerated the numbers as well. Thousands of families here in America and possibly tens of thousands more around the world whose family member died from a car accident, a drug overdose, cancer, suicide, hiking accident, heart attack, brain hemorrhage, or gunshot wound (to name a few) were surprised to read that their loved one's death certificate had the reason for death listed as "COVID." Suddenly, with the THUGS in control, every death became a Covid death.[38]

The medical community and big Pharma are very aware of the law on the books that stipulates no "Emergency Use Authorization" for a vaccine will be granted, if there are other repurposed medicines that have shown to be effective against the pathogen.[39] This explains why government, big Pharma, Doctors, Hospitals, Pharmacists, Media, and big Tech (who've become globalist controlled) ferociously monitored and shut down every informative post on mainstream and social media that shared the positive outcomes from these repurposed drugs, and put measures in place through doctors and pharmacies to prevent their purchase—because this stood in the way of big Pharma making billions on these experimental injections and threatened the execution of their years in the planning, Global coup.[40,41]

They threatened every courageous doctor who was using this life-saving protocol and experiencing great results with their patients, by removing their hospital privileges and threatening to remove their licenses. The THUGS tyrannical control of all forms of media and government soon metastasized to silencing *every voice of truth.*[42,43]

SATAN ALWAYS OVERPLAYS HIS HAND

They canceled and silenced every individual they could find and de-platformed organizations and ministries trying to get the truth out to the public (or merely exercising their Constitutionally protected first amendment rights by speaking their truth regarding other issues). It was at this point the globalist THUGS showed their hand. They wickedly chose *money* over morality, *self* over humanity, evil over good, and *Satan* over GOD![44,45,46] The righteous, however, are required to warn the wicked. (Ezekiel 3:18 NASB95) reads, "If I warn the wicked, saying, 'You are under the penalty of death,' but you fail to deliver the warning, they will die in their sins. And I will hold you responsible for their deaths."

Out of obedience to God's Word, I choose to not only warn the wicked, but to forgive those who have willfully done evil against their fellowman. I pray for them to turn from their wicked ways, repent, and receive Jesus Christ as their Lord and Savior. Salvation is for *anyone* who chooses to receive Jesus' sacrificial gift that He purchased by His blood on the cross.

Now, because of Jesus' death, burial, and resurrection, we have been given a divine inheritance and eternal life in heaven! Here are some of God's multiple warnings to the wicked.

SCRIPTURE REFERENCES

"I, the Lord, will punish the world for its evil and the wicked for their sin. I will crush the arrogance of the proud and humble the pride of the mighty" (Isaiah 13:11, NLT).

"Evil brings death to the wicked, and those who hate the righteous will be punished" (Psalm 34:21, CSB).

"Woe to the wicked! Disaster is upon them! They will be paid back for what their hands have done" (Isaiah 3:11, NIV).

"He will rain down blazing coals and burning sulfur on the wicked, punishing them with scorching winds. For the righteous Lord loves justice. The virtuous will see his face" (Psalm 11:6–7, NLT).

"He who justifies the wicked, and he who condemns the just, Both of them alike are an abomination to the Lord" (Proverbs 17:15, NKJV).

"Give them the punishment they so richly deserve! Measure it out in proportion to their wickedness. Pay them back for all their evil deeds! Give them a taste of what they have done to others" (Psalm 28:4, NLT).

"WHEN YOU TAKE A SECRET BRIBE, YOUR ACTIONS REVEAL YOUR TRUE CHARACTER, FOR YOU PERVERT THE WAYS OF JUSTICE."

—PROVERBS 17:23, TPT

"Then he will say to those on his left, 'Depart from me, you who are cursed, into the eternal fire prepared for the devil and his angels" (Matthew 25:41, NIV).

"Righteous people will be rewarded for their own righteous behavior, and wicked people will be punished for their own wickedness. But if wicked people turn away from all their sins and begin to obey my decrees and do what is just and right, they will surely live and not die" (Ezekiel 18:20–21, NLT).

DO WE REALLY GAIN FROM "GAIN OF FUNCTION?"

Gain of function is a moral and ethical grenade. Its benign sounding title is intentionally deceptive. Globalist talking heads play down the sinister potential for pathogens to be intentionally genetically altered with the sole purpose to be used in bio-warfare against hostile, aggressive nations.[47,48,49]

Those working in these top-secret bio-laboratories here, in Ukraine, and around the world (as morally compromised as they may be), would probably be the first to tell you that they didn't sign up for these genetically altered viruses to be released on the entire global population and *especially their own family*! Secret laboratory experimentation to increase the transmissibility and/or virulence of a pathogen, making it lethal to humans, especially when it wasn't beforehand is a moral and ethical travesty. Time will unfortunately prove the Covid-19 virus, straight from the Wuhan Lab (and possibly American labs before that), is the satanic globalists' "exhibit-A" in their wicked plan toward depopulation and destroying mankind for profit.[50]

TYRANNICAL HUMANITY–HATERS USURPING GOD'S SOVEREIGNTY

Sir, my concern is not whether God is on our side;
my greatest concern is to be on God's side,
for God is always right.

—ABRAHAM LINCOLN

We've been taken over by THUGS! There are many derogatory names, all true, that could be used to describe these Satanically inspired mass-murdering globalists. I believe my acronym THUGS seems to accurately describe the Tyrannical, Humanity-Haters, Usurping God's Sovereignty.[51] The Bible warns us of the evil we would face in the last days. The globalist Thugs openly boast of their evil plans before carrying them out. They publicly reveal their sinister intentions as a type of sadistic badge of honor. Based on public interviews and speeches given at the WEF, TED Talk forums, and U.N. International Conferences on Population, their diabolical plans have been in the works for decades.[52,53,54]

Evil that once operated in the shadows under the cloak of secrecy, is now *openly* and brazenly paraded in the light of day. The only way to understand this kind of 2 Timothy 3 demonic behavior (unholy, brutal, despisers of good), much less try to explain it, is to consider the source! Now, after witnessing the deliberate and escalating devastation that has been repeatedly heaped upon the citizens of the world by the globalist THUGS, the bad actors described in this prophetic scripture have come to life in front of our eyes. Let's look at this again: "But know this, that in the last days perilous times will come: For men will be lovers of themselves, lovers of money, boasters, proud, blasphemers, disobedient to parents, unthankful, unholy, unloving, unforgiving, slanderers, without self-control, brutal, despisers of good, traitors, head-strong haughty, lovers of pleasure rather than lovers of God, having a form of godliness but denying its power. And from such people turn away!" (2 Timothy 3:1-5, NKJV).

God, in His infinite mercy, is warning His children of what to look out for in the last days, so that we will not be deceived. His Holy Word is a powerful beacon of light shining on what lays ahead, so that we will not be caught off-guard or fall into the trap of the enemy. We take courage in our loving heavenly Father's powerful promises of wisdom, hope, peace, courage, and strength.

SCRIPTURE REFERENCES

"These things I have spoken to you so that in Me you may have peace. In the world you have tribulation, but take courage; I have overcome the world" (John 16:33, NASB).

"I pray that your hearts will be flooded with light so that you can understand the confident hope he has given to those he called—his holy people who are his rich and glorious inheritance" (Ephesians 1:18, NLT).

"The Ten Commandments were given so that all could see the extent of their failure to obey God's laws. But the more we see our sinfulness, the more we see God's abounding grace forgiving us" (Romans 5:20, TLB).

"I can do all things through Christ who strengthens me" (Philippians 4:13, NKJV).

THE PLANNED DEMISE OF AMERICA

Truth can be stranger than fiction. The person who is responsible as the funder of bioweapons research on gain of function bat coronaviruses at the Wuhan Institute of Virology, was chosen to be the chief Covid-19 spokesperson to the American public, in cooperation with the CDC, NIH, NIAID, WHO and others.[55,56]

The chief spokesperson, along with these governmental health organizations (the first three who were originally formed to *safeguard* the health of American citizens but have now been systemically corrupted by money and politics),[57,58] operate with governmental authority to restrict the personal freedoms of every human being in America. The THUG-serving phrase "follow the science" has been daily verbally vomited to the amenable public, despite their irrational reversals of opinions and/or questionable extensions of lockdowns to elicit more fear.[59]

They arbitrarily imposed mask wearing on adults, children, and preschool toddlers; closed and bankrupted businesses by deeming them "non-essential," (except for liquor stores and marijuana dispensaries, whom they deemed "essential"). Larger, high traffic, big box corporations could stay open. They insanely kept children home from school for months on end. Then they determined parents could go back to work but at the same time, school children could not.[60,61,62,63,64]

Local and state governments tyrannically prohibited and limited religious gatherings and worship services, while openly promoting and celebrating the large crowds of (paid) anarchists, rioters, looters, and arsonists who attacked police officers, damaged property, and burned down buildings on a nightly basis, for months.

They prohibited and limited holiday, funeral, and family gatherings, and ultimately imposed governmental threats of loss of livelihood through un-constitutional vaccine mandates on everyone they could, to force them to get the experimental and in many cases lethal, clot shot.

"Blessed is the one who perseveres under trial because, having stood the test, that person will receive the crown of life that the Lord has promised to those who love him" (James 1:12, NIV).

These wolves in sheep's clothing stood to gain billions along with big pharma's multiple billions, when the decades in the planning "plandemic" and corresponding experimental injections were heavily promoted and forced on the public through extreme coercion, bullying, and threat of job loss.[65] The more sustained fear they could induce through the cooperation of the corrupt mainstream media and the big tech overlords, the more money they stood to gain through these so-called vaccines.[66]

Above all, don't lie to yourself. The man who lies to himself and listens to his own lie comes to a point that he cannot distinguish the truth within him, or around him, and so loses all respect for himself and for others. And having no respect he ceases to love.

—FYODOR DOSTOEVSKY,
author of *The Brothers Karamazov*

The extremely brave whistleblowers who pointed out the sickening (money-link) collusion *between* big Pharma, the Government, medical (doctors, hospitals, pharmacists), big tech, and the mainstream media, were immediately discredited, de-platformed (canceled and silenced), their lives were threatened, and they were labeled conspiracy theorists. Tragically, catastrophic death, injury, and following the money-trail have proven the courageous whistleblowers' assessments of the wicked cabal of government-pharma-medical-big tech-media collusion and corruption to be correct.[67,68,69]

DID THE GLOBALIST THUGS TAKE THE VACCINE?
(YOU BE THE JUDGE)

It's not like we didn't see this coming. We've been warned by the global de-populationists for years. Several world renown physicians, virologists, epidemiologists, and vaccinologists (including a big Pharma scientist who helped create the mRNA Covid-19 vaccine technology and has now become a whistleblower), have spoken up regarding the toxic ingredients in these experimental injections and the short-term and long-term damage it will inflict on untold billions. Many who have taken the jab, including emergency doctors who have witnessed the deadly effects of this lethal experimental injection, now regret it![70,71,72,73]

Whether taken by choice or by coercion, the damaging side effects include: erratic blood cell clumping (blood cells sticking together causing blood clots, heart attacks, and strokes); irreversible RNA/DNA gene altering therapy (the first world-wide injection that moves the population toward the globalists' agenda for transhumanism)[74]; pathogenic priming which weaponizes spike proteins causing cytokine storms (where the immune system attacks itself when exposed to the next vaccine/booster producing variant); ADE (antibody dependent enhancement) increasing immunity erosion and ultimately immunity collapse leading to AIDS (or VAIDS[75] vaccine-induced auto-immune deficiency syndrome) resulting in escalating cancers, Alzheimer's, ALS, and Parkinson's; reproductive infertility (sterilization) and if pregnant while getting the injection, sterilization passed down to your child (if the child wasn't spontaneously aborted, as many thousands have been)[76]; and graphene oxide nano-particles with magnetic conductive qualities many scientists believe can/will be detrimentally manipulated by the pervasively numerous and powerful 5G, 6G. . .etc. cell towers.[77]

THEY WICKEDLY CHOSE

MONEY OVER MORALITY,

SELF OVER HUMANITY,

EVIL OVER GOOD, AND

SATAN OVER GOD!

CHAPTER SIX:

THE OPEN ROAD EXPOSED

WE HAVE
ENTERED INTO THE
END-TIMES WAR OF
GOOD AND EVIL
THAT THE BIBLE
PREDICTED WOULD
HAPPEN.

6

THE OPEN ROAD
EXPOSED

We are grateful to the *Washington Post, The New York Times, Time Magazine*, and other great publications whose directors have attended our meetings and respected their promises of discretion for almost forty years. It would have been impossible for us to develop our plan for the world if we had been subjected to the lights of publicity during those years. But the world is now more sophisticated and prepared to march towards a world government. The supranational sovereignty of an intellectual elite and world bankers is surely preferable to the national auto-determination practiced in past centuries. [78]

— DAVID ROCKEFELLER

The "national auto-determination" that Rockefeller is so obviously threatened by, happens to be our Constitutionally protected First Amendment rights. To understand the globalist THUGS endgame, we must first look at how other nations have fallen to communistic globalist control. This was accomplished through sustained fear and lockdowns; intimidation; coercion; manufactured anarchy and incitement to violence; manufactured wars; loss of Constitutionally protected personal rights, property, jobs, and self-determination (choices); weakening of the family, community, government, and the education system through immorality by removing God; inciting racial/gender strife and division; declaring Marshall law; and finally, the removal of self-protection (guns).

For decades we've witnessed the globalists' unapologetically avowing their genocidal depopulation wish-list. With a wicked smirk during a Ted Talk[79], they calmly reveal that this will be accomplished through vaccines, health care, and reproductive health services. It sounds positively altruistic, until these deceptive misnomers are exposed for their true meaning. . .timed-release lethal injections, abortion, and sterilization.[80,81]

French Virologist and Nobel Prize Winner Dr. Luc Montagnier was asked his thoughts on the Covid-19 mass vaccination compared to treatments that work and aren't expensive:

It's an enormous mistake, isn't it?

A scientific error as well as a medical error.

It is an unacceptable mistake. The history books will

show that because it is the vaccination that

is creating the variants. For the China virus,

there are antibodies, created by the vaccine.

What does the virus do? Does it die or find

another solution? The new variants are a

production and result from the vaccination.

You see it in each country, it's the same: the

curve of vaccination is followed by the curve of

deaths. I'm following this closely and I am doing

experiments at the Institute with patients who

became sick with Corona after being vaccinated.

I will show you that they are creating the

variants that are resistant to the vaccine.[82]

—PROF. LUC MONTAGNIER,
2008 Nobel Laureate
(now deceased under suspicious circumstances).

The Satan-inspired globalist THUGS have devised the perfect plan; a toxic virus and a time-released health destroying injection meant just for us (but not for them). They unleash a lab-designed bioweapon on the unsuspecting public (in which our tax dollars pay for), followed by a lethal vaccine that the public will stand in line for, after being emotionally whipped into a frenzy for weeks and months of 24/7 fear mongering. The virus in the vaccinated, trying to stay alive (which is what viruses do, "Biology 101") mutates into another variant, requiring a new vaccine. Each new vaccination/booster creates a new variant, which in turn requires a new booster and so on.[83,84]

Have you noticed how the so-called
"experts" are usually incompetent morons?
We have experts in finance who don't know that
printing trillions of dollars causes inflation.
We have experts in education and psychology
who think mutilating the genitals of children
is something to celebrate in the name of
"pride." We have experts in diplomacy who
think Russia has no right to its own national
interests. And we have experts in science
and medicine whose vaccines are so deadly,
they have to resort to censorship and paid
propaganda to cover up all the vaccine deaths.[85]

—MIKE ADAMS
author, Environmental Scientist

Big Pharma has greedily profited billions of dollars off the death and suffering from the global population and has no intention of allowing this financial windfall revolving door to stop.[86,87,88,89] As we're inspired by the Holy Spirit to look at the big picture through the eyes of wisdom, clarity, and discernment from God's prophetic Word, many informed believers in Christ have rightly declared, "We have entered into the end-times war of good and evil that the Bible predicted would happen!" It has been there in the Word of God, for anyone to read. To put it simply, the Satanic globalist THUGS have declared war on humanity!

> *If you can't explain it simply, you*
> *don't understand it well enough.*
> —ALBERT EINSTEIN

MY GOVERNMENT WOULDN'T INTENTIONALLY HARM ME—WOULD THEY?

This question only pertains to countries whose governments are not Communistic; in which case the brutality of its citizens is self-evident. In years past, the answer to this question would have been entirely dependent upon who was in power at the time. Unfortunately, from 2020 going forward, the world population including the United States has witnessed an organized, centralized, and demonized Globalist coup on humanity that has locked in almost every country's government within its evil clutches and control. While we've been sleeping for decades, the THUGS met in their secret clubs (The order of Skull and Bones, Freemasons, The German Thule Society, The Illuminati, CFR (Council on Foreign Relations), Bilderberg Group, WEF (World Economic Forum), the Club of Rome have with unified purpose, strategically plotted and planned their Satanically inspired takeover and depopulation of the world.

SCRIPTURE REFERENCES

"My people are destroyed from lack of knowledge. "Because you have rejected knowledge, I also reject you as my priests; because you have ignored the law of your God, I also will ignore your children" (Hosea 4:6, NIV).

How will God's elect be deceived?

"For false messiahs and false prophets will appear and perform great signs and wonders to deceive, if possible, even the elect. See, I have told you ahead of time" (Matthew 24:24, NIV).

Cognitive dissonance is the scientific term that explains our conscious ability to override what our brain is telling us to be true. For example, an attacker approaches us with a weapon and tells us if we give him our money, he won't hurt us, when our panicked brain is screaming, turn around and run! We override our brain and do what he says and the outcome is? Another example is an unwanted pregnancy. Your brain might be saying, "don't have an abortion, you'll be taking the innocent life of your own child, yet you override your brain and take what you think is the easy way out—and the outcome is?

One final example: You're hearing the same message everywhere, repeated by everyone on every media platform from government officials to celebrities, but something inside you is saying, "No, this isn't right! As an American citizen I shouldn't be forced to take an unproven, experimental injection against my will and my Constitutionally protected First Amendment Rights!" Because your job is on the line, that important vacation is coming up, family and friends are obediently doing what they are told and pressuring you to do so as well. You override your brain and follow the crowd—and the outcome is?

Cognitive dissonance: *psychological conflict resulting from incongruous beliefs and attitudes held simultaneously.*

—MERRIAM-WEBSTER DICTIONARY

"THE PSYCHOLOGICAL TENSION THAT OCCURS WHEN ONE HOLDS MUTUALLY EXCLUSIVE BELIEFS OR ATTITUDES AND THAT OFTEN MOTIVATES PEOPLE TO MODIFY THEIR THOUGHTS OR BEHAVIORS IN ORDER TO REDUCE THE TENSION."

—DICTIONARY BY FARLEX

SHEEP WANT TO BE TAKEN CARE OF

"The Lord is my shepherd; I have all that I need. He lets me rest in green meadows; he leads me beside peaceful streams. He renews my strength. He guides me along right paths, bringing honor to his name. Even when I walk through the darkest valley, I will not be afraid, for you are close beside me. Your rod and your staff protect and comfort me" (Psalm 23:1-4, NLT).

"My people have been lost sheep; their shepherds have led them astray and caused them to roam on the mountains. They wandered over mountain and hill and forgot their own resting place. Whoever found them devoured them; their enemies said, 'We are not guilty, for they sinned against the Lord, their true pasture, the Lord, the hope of their fathers" (Jeremiah 50:6-7, NIV).

Are we experiencing what no other generation before us has endured, an *intentional* global plague? When you dig deep, you will find Scientists who are now saying the 1918 pandemic of Spanish Flu was neither from Spain, nor was it the flu.[90] Whether we are experiencing the first intentional global pandemic or history repeating itself, our brain might be in denial as to the accumulation of facts that have been coming to light (despite the prolonged silencing campaign by government, big tech, and mainstream media). World renowned scientists and physicians that have nothing to gain and *everything* to lose by coming forward are saying not to take the vaccine, because it wasn't tested on humans, only animals and the clinical trials show that all the animals died.[91,92,93,94,95]

Humanity has unwittingly become the "Phase 2" clinical trials, and it doesn't look good. We have newscasters, athletes, celebrities, friends and family, and now small children falling ill and dying before our eyes with blood clots, strokes, heart attacks, myocarditis, pericarditis, auto-immune diseases, cancers, tremors, seizures, and we can't seem to open our eyes and figure out what the common denominator is.

Our brain has a survival mechanism that allows us to make even *detrimental* choices and then be able to justify to ourselves and those around us we made the right choice. All sheep desire to hear the protective voice of their shepherd. We may choose to never rest in the green meadows (the place of rest and peace) that Jesus has for us or out of rebellion choose to wander from His protective care, but there is an indisputably divine longing within each of us to be cared for by our Creator, Savior, and Great Shepherd. In the absence of Jesus leading and guiding our lives, we will follow *anyone* that offers safety and shelter, especially wolves dressed in sheep's clothing.

> *If people aren't governed by religious faith, there will never be enough laws to restrain evil. Faith provides self-restraint as guided by the conscience.*
>
> —KELLY J SHACKELFORD,
> President, CEO and Chief Counsel, First Liberty

The brave scientists and physicians who spoke up and said these injections won't prevent infection, or transmission were ridiculed, de-platformed (canceled and silenced), and their lives were threatened. Time has proven these extremely courageous souls to be correct in their assessment.[96] The writing is on the wall! The evil that so easily corrupts the heart of man, leaves a trail and it's usually a money trail. For this money trail to keep flowing for the THUGS who are now in control of most of the world's governments, they know they must never stop the constant mind-control or brainwashing of the masses. The scientific term is "mass formation psychosis," having been successfully used by evil despots in times past. This can only be accomplished by the unrelenting fear mongering that the globalists exert over governments through the corrupt mainstream media portals they control. Have we learned nothing from history?[97]

Of course, the obvious example of mass formation is Germany in the 1930's and 40's. How could the German people who were highly educated, very liberal in the classic sense; western thinking people. . .how could they go so crazy and do what they did to the Jews? How could this happen? To a civilized people? A leader of a mass formation movement will use the platform to continue to pump the group with new information to focus on. In the case of Covid-19, I like to use the term "fear porn." Leaders, through mainstream media and government channels continuously feed the "beast" with more messaging that focus and further hypnotize their adherents.[98]

—ROBERT W. MALONE, MD,
Physician, Scientist

Those in positions of power with blackened hearts have boasted, "Never let a good crisis go to waste!" [99] The radical communists and billionaire socialists that comprise the Satanic globalist THUGS, believe that their plan will achieve all their purposes. This comes as no surprise to those who study the Word of God and understand end-time Bible prophecy. The book of Revelation prophetically speaks of the wickedness of the last days that will be far greater than any other time, of deceivers that will deliberately manipulate the minds of the trusting and gullible, and the tumultuous events leading to a "One-World" government that demonically controls every human on the face of the earth. This "one-world" positioning ushers in the Antichrist who will ultimately force the whole world to take his Satanic "mark of the Beast," or lose their life.

Through the Word of God, Believers in Christ or "the Bride of Christ" have been given the divine assurance that our "Bridegroom" will return for His bride (the Rapture of the saints) and take us to our eternal heavenly home. Although some believe this will occur before the seven-year tribulation period begins and others believe this will take place during the first half of the tribulation, the ultimate goal is to be ready whenever our Bridegroom returns for His bride.

"Let us rejoice and be glad and give him glory! For the wedding of the Lamb has come, and his bride has made herself ready" (Revelation 19:7, NIV).

'JAB REMORSE'

If you want to make a conservative angry—tell them a lie. If you want to make a liberal angry—tell them the truth.

—ANONYMOUS

It is devastating to the core beliefs of a civilized society when we are forced to acknowledge that our government, along with big Pharma, has become *the biggest drug dealer on the planet*.[100,101,102] A drug dealer's modus operandi is predictably maleficent: they care nothing about their "users;" they will do anything to get you to try their product; they are indifferent to the fact that you could overdose and die; and they count on you becoming addicted. The only thing they do care about is not getting caught and they will do anything (including lie, cheat, steal, threaten, bribe, slander, and murder) to prevent that from happening.

Many are waking up to the fact they have been lied to. Not by a telemarketer over the phone, not by someone selling a faulty item over the internet, not by someone "catfishing" on a dating App, and not by another crooked politician lying to get our vote, but by our own government (the elected ones who swore to uphold the Constitution and defend human life). This time, their lies not only affect our freedom and our finances but go well beyond to the maniacal damage and devastation of a time-released lethal injection aimed against anyone who believed their lies or was coerced into it.

Many are waking up to the insidious betrayal our government has perpetrated on its own citizens and are filled with remorse for allowing their bodies to be jabbed with an unknown, untested, toxic substance.

Modern psychotherapy relates the human emotions that result from a deep and personal betrayal as being: first shock, then denial, anger, depression, and finally acceptance. If you have been affected by this lie, it is important for you to understand that it is not over, and they have not won! According to America's Frontline Covid-19 Critical Care (FLCCC) Alliance, there are steps that can still be taken to help your body fight the vaccine damage. The first step is DO NOT take any more vaccines or boosters!

Most importantly, is our acknowledgment that one of the Names of our heavenly Father is Jehovah Rapha "God our Healer." His Word tells us, "He is no respecter of persons." When Jesus walked among us here on earth, He healed all who had faith in Him. He didn't just seek out the righteous to heal, but He healed all who came to him, and He still heals today!

The Bible tells us that because of the finished work on the cross, Jesus' blood not only saved and redeemed us from an eternity in hell, but purchased our healing our healing and deliverance from every bondage as well. When we accept Jesus into our heart, our sin debt has been lovingly "PAID IN FULL!" Going forward it is imperative that we keep our eyes on Jesus. Institutions, agencies and charitable organizations will not save us; ministers, priests, rabbis, and the Pope will not save us; our education, job, investments, and bank accounts will not save us; and certainly, our government will not save us. Our only *Savior* is Jesus, who willingly died and rose again so that we might be reconciled back to our heavenly Father and receive eternal life.

LOOK WHERE THE OPEN ROAD HAS LED US!

The old saying, "If we refuse to learn from the mistakes of the past, we're destined to repeat them," is pointing its "I told you so" finger at us now. History has shown us over and over that "Absolute power corrupts Absolutely," and corrupt governments cannot be trusted. Have you ever wondered why many Jews during World War II barely escaped with their lives, while thousands of others were rounded up and died during the Holocaust? It came down to the simple fact of choosing to believe, or not believe a lie. Here is one of the lies they were told by Adolph Eichmann, one of Hitler's henchmen:

All Jews listen up! At last it can be reported
to you that the Russians are advancing on our
eastern front. I apologize for the hasty way we
brought you into our protection. Unfortunately,
there was little time to explain. You have nothing
to worry about. We want only the best for you.
You will leave here shortly and be sent to very fine
places indeed. You will work there, your wives
will stay at home, and your children will go to
school. You will have wonderful lives. We will all
be terribly crowded on the trains, but the journey
is short. Men, please keep families together
and board the rail cars in an orderly manner.
Quickly now, my friends, we must hurry![103]

—ADOLPH EICHMANN

They say hindsight is 20/20. We literally now have the accurate perspective of looking back since 2020 at the trail of tears deliberately inflicted on the world's population by our own governments and the puppet-master THUGS controlling them. We have witnessed with our own eyes for the first time in our lifetime, a demonically orchestrated event involving every person on earth! All of the horrific holocausts perpetrated on cultures and civilizations from the dawn of time, may ultimately pale in comparison to this planned global annihilation.

The globalist THUGS rollout of their "Round-(1)" multi-pronged approach of sustained fear, isolation, and destruction of lives, livelihoods, and economies while simultaneously controlling the narrative through every major mainstream media and social media outlet was moderately successful in their eyes, although they were not satisfied with *only* millions of lives that were lost. They want that number to be in the billions, which is why they intend to keep rolling out one increasingly lethal plague after another (primarily dispersed at international events) and have an equally lethal vaccine waiting in the wings, to profit from the devastation.

The THUGS conveniently blame it on the un-vaccinated, because causing division between spouses, family, friends, co-workers, and teammates not only applies pressure on those unwilling to participate in their depopulation plan but also creates a scapegoat for the sick and angry to blame, instead of the real perpetrators.[104,105] So far, everything is going according to plan. This plan has been in the works for quite some time and is easily accessible for all who care to look for it and read. The modern-day THUGS draw extensively from "The Communist Manifesto" by Karl Marx and Friedrich Engels and their game plan has been carefully laid out, courtesy of the Bilderbergers.

2005 BILDERBERG CONFERENCE
(PLANS TO DESTABILIZE THE WORLD)

1) Create subversion from within

2) Maintain a state of perpetual imbalance

3) Degeneracy and toxic cultural decay (for psychological warfare)

4) Creative Destruction (gaining ground/ control through manufactured crisis)

5) Technocracy/Media (are members of these clubs and take their marching orders from the Trilateral Commission, CFR, and the Bilderberg Group)

6) Centralized control of the masses

7) Centralization of all education (parental control transferred to designated surrogates)

8) Zero growth society—in economy (stagnation), and population (more deaths than births)

9) Revolutionary movements (effective tools for destruction)[106]

HOW DO WE OVERCOME?

Bible prophecy foretells the seven-year Tribulation period, which will be the last seven years on earth, culminating with the cataclysmic events leading to the battle of Armageddon in Israel. Everyone still alive from the THUGS depopulation efforts will be forced to take the "mark of the beast" (the mark of the Antichrist), which most likely will be a digital tattoo or digitally implanted chip on every human being's right hand or forehead. This will be necessary for the purposes of buying and selling and no one will be allowed to eat or exist without it.

Once the mark is taken, their allegiance to the Satanically controlled Antichrist is sealed and irrevocable. You could say that the Covid-19 experimental injection was a trial run for preparing the masses to obediently fall in line to receive the mark. You don't have to go far to see the mass psychosis already on display; regrettably, through their woke methods of psychological incentivization, many have witnessed the hateful and loathsome way the brainwashed (both in Germany and now today), have easily *turned on* and *turned in* their own family, friends, neighbors, co-workers, and teammates who exercised critical thinking and refused to march in lockstep with the tyrannical agenda.[107,108,109]

> "He required everyone—small and great, rich, and poor, free and slave—to be given a mark on the right hand or on the forehead. And no one could buy or sell anything without that mark, which was either the name of the beast or the number representing his name. Wisdom is needed here. Let the one with understanding solve the meaning of the number of the beast, for it is the number of a man. His number is 666" (Revelation 13:16–18, NLT).

The cataclysmic end-time battle between Life and death, Good and evil, Truth and lies, and Freedom and slavery is ultimately between God and Satan for the souls of mankind before time has run out! Only those who accept Jesus into their heart and refuse the mark will be saved.

> "By his divine power, God has given us everything we need for living a godly life. We have received all of this by coming to know him, the one who called us to himself by means of his marvelous glory and excellence. And because of his glory and excellence, he has given us great and precious promises. These are the promises that enable you to share his divine nature and escape the world's corruption caused by human desires" (2 Peter 1:3–4, NLT).

This globalist trifecta will not easily go away, nor do they plan for it to. First, it will ultimately enable them to remove the roadblocks of strong and stubborn nations (by weakening America, among others) that wouldn't fall in line with their globalist agenda; giving them control of the world's governments, resources, and people. This will ultimately solve their dilemma of capturing complete *control* of every human being on the planet physically, socially, and financially through the potential use of a digital implant.

Second, it also accomplishes their diabolical agenda that through abortion; sterilization; lab-created bio-warfare plagues; experimental vaccines (time-released lethal injections); 5G radiation sickening the public (especially those contaminated with graphene oxide from the Covid-19 injections); toxic air polluting aluminum/barium chemtrails to manipulate weather patterns, and stratospheric sun-blocking chemicals (under the guise of protection from global warming) sickening both humans and animals, contaminating water reservoirs, and destroying plant life;[110] toxic contaminants added to our drinking water (fluoride—a neurotoxin and endocrine disruptor), and toxins in our soil contaminating our food supply (while we still have a food supply) through carcinogenic pesticides, insecticides, and GMO) they wickedly expect to depopulate the world by several billion! [111,112,113,114]

Third, the continuance of creating global fear and panic, aided by the corrupt big tech and mainstream media (silencing every voice and opinion but their own), works to their extreme *financial* benefit! Fear mongering by the media on a 24/7 basis, creates an environment where it becomes easy to control the herd of fearful, uninformed sheep toward Pharma's latest, greatest vaccine "miracle." [115,116 117,118,119,120]

Life-altering and life-ending ingredients in these injections, along with the unending stream of future injections will undoubtedly be trotted out and heavily promoted by the trendiest celebrity du'jour for the current "plague" that has been unleashed into the unsuspecting public. These "death by injections" are now being unconstitutionally forced on the global population without informed consent for to have informed consent, you must be *informed* and made aware of all the possible consequences! [121,122,123]

Covid-19 Vaccine Induced Acquired Immune Deficiency Syndrome, or VAIDS, appears to be one of the more serious long-term adverse effects caused by the injections. In essence, the shots are destroying people's immune systems over time, leaving them prone to infections of all kinds. . .with several billion people around the planet having taken these AIDS-causing vaccines, it means we're looking at a global explosion of AIDS diagnoses that makes people extremely vulnerable to common infections such as colds and flu. As a "solution" to all this, the same vaccine corporations are about to roll out "AIDS vaccines" to treat the very problem they caused. [124]

—MIKE ADAMS,
Environmental Scientist

All the wicked collaborators involved in silencing the truth, have the blood of potentially billions on their hands. Whether they silenced the truth by blocking or de-platforming those brave enough to speak out; or by taking an active role in covering up the many vaccine deaths and injuries that are continuing to occur; or by blocking the dispensing of time-honored medications that have been proven effective in fighting/preventing viruses and death; or deliberately sending infected patients back to nursing homes/care centers to spread the disease to the elderly; or the heinous governmental financial incentivization programs with doctors and hospitals (administered by the staff) to put their patients on certain organ damaging and/or coma inducing medications which accelerated the need for a ventilator; and last, but not least the Satan-inspired globalist THUGS, who've spent years working out every possible scenario that would impede their diabolical "plandemic" of depopulation and world control. They *all* share in the horrific murder and injury of the global population and will one day bow their knee before the Creator of the Universe and must give an account for their evil actions before their ultimate punishment begins, an eternity in hell.[125,126,127,128,129,130]

"So that at the name of Jesus every knee should bow, in heaven and on earth and under the earth, and every tongue confess that Jesus Christ is Lord to the glory of God the Father" (Philippians 2:10, ESV).

I pray that time DOES NOT prove these courageous scientists to be correct in their assessment of the long-term effects on the human body, because the result will be devastation and mass-depopulation on a scale we have never seen before! The fact that the shots don't *prevent* infection or transmission seems miniscule by comparison; however, government and big Pharma's insidious work around and *last resort* sales pitch (this time) is that the shot will lessen the symptoms, which is initially true. Unfortunately, many scientists predict that the temporary immunity boost is short-lived, and the spike proteins within the vaxxed have now become weaponized *against their own* immune system, to attack at the next virus appearance.[131,132,133]

There were many who spoke up against the government's unconstitutional edicts, the unlawful trampling of our First-Amendment rights by canceling and silencing free speech, calling out the elected officials for promoting a socialist agenda and the unlawful shuttering of businesses and churches, while unjustly allowing liquor stores, marijuana dispensaries, and big box stores to stay open. These brave souls were called conspiracy theorists, bullied by their local and state governments, fined for trying to earn a living, feed their families, or minister to their congregations—and their social media accounts were de-platformed (canceled and silenced). Time has proven these brave souls, business owners, and ministers of the gospel correct in their assessment. Many months of data collected from countries around the world overwhelmingly show that the shutdowns did not stop or even slow the spread of the virus, but indeed emboldened the spread of government tyranny and control.

> *One of the greatest lessons of the past five centuries*
> *in Europe and America is this: acute crisis*
> *contributes to boosting the power of the state.*
> *It's always been the case, and there is no reason why*
> *it should be different with the Covid-19 pandemic.*[134]
>
> —KLAUS SCHWAB, executive chairman,
> founder World Economic Forum

You have it "straight from the horse's mouth!" The globalists have long understood that if you want to boost the power and control of the state (tyrannical power grab), you must create an "acute crisis," through wars, terrorist attacks, and pandemics. Their "gaslighting" pattern is to openly declare their global intentions, while attacking and labeling those who confront them on these same intentions as "conspiracy theorists." I've heard it said that in the future, it's probably more accurate for the God-hating globalists and their media minions to call "conspiracy theories" what they really are, "spoiler alerts!"

In this country, we pledge allegiance to the flag of the *United* States of America. We go on to say, "and to the republic for which it stands, one nation under God, *indivisible,* with liberty and justice for all." Sadly, by all accounts we are no longer a nation under God and have become a country divided and split down the center on so many vital issues. The conflicts, racial strife, divisions, and the spiritual waywardness our nation and every nation around the world are struggling with, can all be exposed to have the same root cause—unbelief and rebellion to God and His Holy Word.

> "My purpose is that they may be encouraged in heart and united in love, so that they may have the full riches of complete understanding, in order that they may know the mystery of God, namely, Christ, in whom are hidden all the treasures of wisdom and knowledge" (Colossians 2:2–4, NIV).

We, as law-abiding citizens, are confronted with Satan-inspired attacks threatening our peace and safety in every area of our lives. This is unfortunately being evidenced on both sides of the law. If we were ever inclined to unite by coming together as a nation and putting our differences aside, wouldn't now be the time?

ALL THE PEOPLE WHO HAVE BEEN VILIFIED ARE CRITICAL THINKERS... IF YOU DON'T TAKE THE MARCHING ORDERS AND YOU QUESTION, YOU'RE VILIFIED AND PUSHED ASIDE, AND THIS IS LITERALLY A CRISIS OF CRITICAL THINKING ACROSS ALL INDUSTRIES.[135]

—EDWARD DOWD,
FORMER BLACKROCK PORTFOLIO MANAGER

WHAT DOES ANARCHY LOOK LIKE?

• On one side: unjust or heavy-handed law enforcement and on the other: the murders of intentionally targeted law enforcement.

• Our Federal Government is fleecing hardworking taxpayers through the insanity of sending billions of our tax money without our approval (which is taxation without representation) to terrorist nations that want America and Israel wiped off the face of the earth. Peace cannot be purchased; evil is only subdued and defeated through strength by a strong military, strong and wise God-fearing governmental leadership, and God-answered prayer!

• Crucial Constitutional Amendments are overturned by judicial activists and Supreme Court Justices, who are hijacking the Justice system and illegally *enacting* law rather than *interpreting* it. This threatens the Constitutionally designated separation of powers (see: "Separation of Church and State, or Separation of Powers?" *Rabbit Trails Redirect*) and turns our Republic into an oligarchy by infringing on the Constitutional Rights of the many, to satisfy the radically liberal wishes of the few.

- Religious Discrimination as a result of this judicial activism, attempts to unconstitutionally marginalize the Conservative and Christian voice. Religious discrimination is openly condoned, by using our tax dollars through government funding of left-leaning organizations and abortion mills that promote murder and immorality. There is implicit bias from the liberal media and big Tech against conservatives, Christian conservatives, and their deeply held Biblical beliefs—as they daily promote a radical, America crippling agenda, while silencing the conservative point of view.

- When Federal laws are unenforced and deliberately broken by radically liberal state Governors, along with government officials who hide behind the false flag of a "sanctuary city." There are *always* reasons behind the insanity we see in government! They do this for the short term: to increase the government dependent and homeless populations, thereby increasing the dependent liberal voting base. They do this for the long term: to expand their radically liberal agendas, thereby, crippling the state (because they are controlled by the globalist THUGS who have a larger agenda)! By releasing violent offenders back onto the streets rather than turning them over to Border Control, Homeland Security, or local sheriffs, they are breaking the laws they swore to uphold and betraying the very citizens they swore to protect. They are committing a treasonous coup against the Federal government, the Constitution, the laws of our land, and its citizens, by turning American cities into lawless, criminal gang safe havens. Wanted felons and undocumented criminals are then free upon release to again rob, rape, and murder law-abiding citizens, placing these elected officials in the same criminal category, thereby making them liable for federal criminal prosecution.

- For many years the radical leftist puppets of the globalist regime have been double-dealing by breaking federal laws through giveaways and enticements that promote and encourage *illegal* immigration and anchor babies. Their clandestine mass social media campaigns to Central America and beyond, encourage caravans of refugees to storm our borders, with millions who have heeded the call and have now illegally found a way into the country. These illegal enticements are for the express purpose of enlarging the liberal voting bloc and weakening the sovereignty of America. Officials then act surprised by the millions of immigrants that now illegally reside in our cities. America has not only benefited but thrived from *legal immigration* and assimilation. This weakening of our borders creates disrespect for our laws, distrust in our government, exponentially higher crime rates, unchecked disease, and social and economic instability. The globalist THUGS ultimate goal is to create economic collapse through the insolvency of our welfare and social services.

• Socialist billionaire funded *community organizers* who use social media to create chaos. Through online sites, they recruit paid rioters to incite violence and exhibit criminal behavior by breaking windows, looting stores until they're stripped bare, destroying vehicles, burning buildings, sucker punching/knocking down elderly passersby, and threatening innocent lives. The anarchist's agenda is to incite fear through the intentional disruption of commerce and transportation and leave their mark by extensively damaged/burned out property. One of our past presidents bragged about being a "community organizer." The anarchists' "paid for" behavior is criminal, and unfortunately, doesn't stop there. The criminals for hire receive not only a schedule for the date and time their misdeeds are to happen, but a map and exact locations of the buildings they are to destroy. The once thriving commercial blocks of local "Mom and Pop" shopkeepers, are quickly turned into a burned and boarded-up ghost town with bottomed-out property values. Soon after (not surprisingly), these depressed properties get bought up, sometimes whole blocks at a time, for pennies on the dollar by *unknown* corporations and entities.

Anarchy will follow when society falls prey to lawlessness, endures the intentional incitements to violence by billionaire socialists, and the relentless undermining of our nation's Constitution. Our own government's liberal, Bible-rejecting and God-hating officials adversely affect and are openly hostile to half of their constituents, America's Bible-believing, law-abiding, and constitutionally conservative citizens.

"AN EVIL MAN IS HELD CAPTIVE BY HIS OWN SINS; THEY ARE ROPES THAT CATCH AND HOLD HIM. HE WILL DIE FOR LACK OF SELF-CONTROL; HE WILL BE LOST BECAUSE OF HIS GREAT FOOLISHNESS."

—PROVERBS 5:22-23, NLT

THE OPEN ROAD OF DECEPTION

Those traveling the open road, who are unaware of what the Word of God actually says, will fall prey to altruistic notions of a godless, humanistic point of view. They naively embrace an open, marshmallow spirituality, which at first is enticing but ultimately offers no divine peace for the present, much less eternal security for the future. At first glance, the allure of the open road is exhilarating, for who wouldn't want to travel in style on the easiest and most scenic route? On closer inspection, however, the festering souls of billions who are filled with emptiness, unrest, desperation, loneliness, anger, and confusion are barreling full speed down the highway towards a dead end.

When a vehicle is filled with the wrong fuel, the engine is damaged and eventually destroyed. A house without a solid foundation will eventually crumble and collapse. A ship with no charted course will eventually end up shipwrecked on the rocky shoreline. *All* of God's beloved creation will eventually self-destruct when separated from our Creator's power, provision, and protection found only in the Bible, His love letter to us.

Without the revelation that first comes from *reading* God's Word, then *believing* and *receiving* it, we fall into denial of our desperate need for redemption, reconciliation, and relationship with our Heavenly Father. The further we get from God's Love, Peace, Light, and Truth, the further we fall into the abyss of darkness and the lies that Satan has repackaged into his own deceptive form of *counterfeit* love, peace, light, and truth.

> "The mind of sinful man is death, but the mind controlled by the Spirit is life and peace; the sinful mind is hostile to God. It does not submit to God's law, nor can it do so. Those controlled by the sinful nature cannot please God" (Romans 8:6–8, NIV).

On this open road there are countless religions, cults, and doctrines espoused by many different cultures that have bits and pieces of truth from the Bible deceptively woven in and through their teachings. Many of these cults, Eastern religions and Eastern New Age derivatives contain just enough distorted scripture to give them an air of legitimacy and a sense of familiarity. The only defense against deception *is to know the Word of God*, "I have hidden your word in my heart that I might not sin against you" (Psalms 119:11 NIV).

"Let no one deceive you with empty words, for because of such things God's wrath comes on those who are disobedient. Therefore do not be partners with them. For you were once darkness, but now you are light in the Lord. Live as children of light (for the fruit of the light consists in all goodness, righteousness, and truth) and find out what pleases the Lord. Have nothing to do with the fruitless deeds of darkness, but rather expose them. For it is shameful even to mention what the disobedient do in secret. But everything exposed by the light becomes visible, for it is light that makes everything visible. This is why it is said: "Wake up, O sleeper, rise from the dead, and Christ will shine on you" (Ephesians 5:6–7, NIV)

SATAN'S FALSE PRODUCT PLACEMENT

The biggest trick up Satan's sleeve is the fact that the Broad Road and the Narrow Road start out in the same vicinity. Truth and deception don't exist as opposites but dwell side by side which allows him to deceive more easily. Satan excels in deceptive *product placement* and disguises his deceptions to sound similar to biblical truth, making the counterfeit seem open and full of light, purpose, revelation, significance, and inspiration.

There are many religions that acknowledge Jesus lived, and that He was a good man, prophet, and teacher. They might even use such names as Jesus Christ, Emmanuel, Messiah, or King of Kings, in the title of their religion, denomination, and reading material. According to the Bible, unless they teach that everyone needs to repent and accept Jesus Christ into their heart as their Lord and Savior, they are deceived and risk deceiving many others with their open, powerless facade of empty words and teachings. Let's identify a few of Satan's favorite open road diversions:

- **Does the God of the Bible tell us of any other way to enter heaven, except through His Son?**

   "Let me clearly state to all of you and to all the people of Israel that he was healed by the powerful name of Jesus Christ the Nazarene, the man you crucified but whom God raised from the dead. For Jesus is the one referred to in the Scriptures, where it says, 'The stone that you builders rejected has now become the cornerstone.' There is salvation in no one else! God has given no other name under heaven by which we must be saved" (Acts 4:10–12, NLT).

• **Does the God of the Bible tell us that if you don't get it right during this lifetime, you can come back again through reincarnation and give it another try?**

"Just as people are destined to die once, and after that to face judgment, so Christ was sacrificed once to take away the sins of many; and he will appear a second time, not to bear sin, but to bring salvation to those who are waiting for him" (Hebrews 9:27–28, NIV).

• **Does the God of the Bible endorse idolatry, child sacrifice, witchcraft, spending time praying to the dead (no matter how saintly or virtuous), or condone our enlisting the help of a medium, fortune teller, or card reader?**

"Let no one be found among you who sacrifices their son or daughter in the fire, who practices divination or sorcery, interprets omens, engages in witchcraft, or casts spells, or who is a medium or spiritist or who consults the dead. Anyone who does these things is detestable to the Lord, and because of these detestable practices the Lord your God will drive out those nations before you. You must be blameless before the Lord your God" (Deuteronomy 18:10–14, NIV).

- **Does the God of the Bible tell us anyone is excluded from receiving Salvation from His Son Jesus?**

"If you confess with your mouth, "Jesus is Lord," and believe in your heart that God raised him from the dead, you will be saved. One believes with the heart, resulting in righteousness, and one confesses with the mouth, resulting in salvation. For the Scripture says, Everyone who believes on him will not be put to shame, since there is no distinction between Jew and Greek, because the same Lord of all richly blesses all who call on him. For everyone who calls on the name of the Lord will be saved" (Romans 10:9–13, CSB).

God is a God of *inclusion* not *exclusion*! His Word tells us He doesn't want anyone to perish but to have eternal life with Him. John 3:16 tells us God loved the world so much that He gave His only Son as a sacrifice for us. God's only requirement for salvation is that we repent of our sins and acknowledge His only beloved Son Jesus as our Lord and Savior. In 2 Thessalonians 2:10, we read: "They perish because they refused to love the truth and so be saved" (KJV). The Bible warns us we perish only when we *choose* to perish!

- **Does the God of the Bible tell us salvation is something that must be earned, strived for, or gained through goodness, self-awareness, self-sacrifice, or self-mutilation?**

  "For you are saved by grace through faith, and this is not from yourselves: it is God's gift—not from works, so that no one can boast. For we are his workmanship, created in Christ Jesus for good works, which God prepared ahead of time for us to do" (Ephesians 2:8–10, CSB).

- **Does the God of the Bible and the Creator of the Universe tell us to go out and kill anyone who refuses to acknowledge Jesus Christ as**

God's only Son? Does the Savior of the world tell us to kill the infidel or anyone who does not believe the way we do? Does the Lamb of God tell us to sacrifice our sons and daughters in the terroristic slaughter of innocent lives to satiate his bottomless pit of hate?

Just the opposite! God loved us with a love so deep and pure, that He gave us His very own Son Jesus Christ to be the sacrificial Lamb, the perfect sinless sacrifice in *our* place. Because of sin we were condemned to an eternity in hell, separated from the One who loves us most, but our loving Savior willingly paid the price for our sins so that we can now walk in love, truth, joy, peace, light, healing, deliverance, and freedom.

When Jesus rose again on the third day, He purchased the security of eternal life for us. The tremendous sacrificial price for our salvation, healing, and deliverance (from every bondage, addiction, or generational curse and iniquity going all the way back to Adam) was purchased on the cross by the blood of Jesus and is *freely* given to anyone who accepts Him into their heart as their Lord and Savior. All we need to do is receive it and declare it over our life. This is what **True Love** looks like.

"For God so loved the world that He gave His one and only Son, that whoever believes in Him shall not perish but have eternal life. For God did not send His Son into the world to condemn the world, but to save the world through Him. Whoever believes in Him is not condemned, but whoever does not believe stands condemned already because he has not believed in the name of God's one and only Son" (John 3:16–18, NIV).

There is no shortage of deception in our world today. Satan is intently focused on distorting biblical Truth, especially within the church. Staying ignorant of what God is speaking to His beloved creation in His Word, is an open invitation to deception. God's Word applies to every area of our lives and is vitally necessary for our earthly success, freedom, and victory. It's easy to accept imitations when you've never experienced the real thing. We eternally sell ourselves short by settling for the open road of the carnal and the quick and easy, rather than acknowledging and embracing God's timeless and everlasting Truth.

REFUSING THE BREAD

Imagine an orphan child, weak from hunger and thirst, stumbling barefoot in the open and desolate wilderness. She discovers a letter that is presented to her on a silver platter. All she needs to do, for her life to change for the better is to accept and open it. Inside is irrefutable evidence of her *true identity,* revealing the name of her Father. He is not only her loving father but a King who longs to provide for His royal child!

This life-changing information would not only ensure she would no longer be a homeless orphan but would legally secure her royal inheritance for eternity. Sadly, the unopened letter is discarded because she could see that it wasn't food, water, shelter, or something to play with. And besides, what if it was from someone with rules for her to obey, telling her she would need to take a bath, wear shoes, or go to school? So the orphan refused the unknown by settling for the familiar. She went back to eating weeds with thorns and drinking water from a polluted puddle, rather than feasting on the royal Bread of Life and drinking the living water flowing from the throne of her Heavenly Father.

"Then Jesus declared, I am the bread of life. He who comes to me will never go hungry, and he who believes in me will never be thirsty" (John 6:35, NIV).

We behave like the orphan child when we refuse God's free gift of salvation. Refusing this extravagantly precious offering is deliberately choosing the deceptive detour that leads *away* from Him. God purchased this precious gift for us through the priceless blood of His only Son Jesus, to redeem us from the clutches of Satan and to reclaim our lost earthly authority that had been transferred to the enemy by our rebellion. The cross changed everything! When we make the choice to refuse Jesus, our Bread of Life, we have sentenced ourselves to spiritual starvation for eternity. *We* have become our own worst enemy when we (whether by default or choice) choose Satan!

IT'S TIME TO MAKE A U-TURN

If you have found yourself on a road other than the narrow road, perhaps you're ready to leave the broad road with the countless and alluring good, crooked, divided, and open road exits and make a U-turn? We must now discover the narrow road that leads to our patient and loving heavenly Father. The world will give you directions to every road *but* the narrow road. They will try to convince you that it's too confining, inconvenient, boring and rigid, or that nobody but a fool would choose the narrow road over the smooth and fast-moving interstate! Nothing could be further from the truth! The dizzying maze of travel opportunities before us, veer off in every direction except the one that leads to LIFE! God's greatest gifts, promises, and eternal blessings come into focus when we *make the decision* to pursue the "narrow road" less traveled.

Without this conscious choice, we are making the biggest mistake of our life, by leaving ourselves wide open to deception, disillusionment, and ultimate destruction. Deception causes our inner compass to malfunction and opens the door to confusion, thus ensuring that we make wrong choices. Deception clouds our judgment, blocks wisdom, and blinds us to the truth. No one in their right mind would refuse to *believe* and *receive* their true identity, royal inheritance, their God-given destiny, and eternal life with their Heavenly Father, Creator and Savior. No one, except someone barreling down the broad road of rebellion.

THE CATACLYSMIC END-TIME BATTLE BETWEEN LIFE AND DEATH, GOOD AND EVIL, TRUTH AND LIES, AND FREEDOM AND SLAVERY IS ULTIMATELY BETWEEN GOD AND SATAN FOR THE SOULS OF MANKIND BEFORE TIME HAS RUN OUT!

CHAPTER SEVEN:

THE

NARROW

ROAD

GOD'S MOST
PRECIOUS GIFTS THAT
HE LONGS TO GIVE
TO HIS CHILDREN
ARE BURIED IN THE
TREASURE CHEST OF
HIS HOLY WORD.

7

THE NARROW ROAD

"But small is the gate and narrow the road
that leads to life, and only a few find it"
(Matthew 7:14, NIV).

This doesn't sound encouraging. Why is the gate small, the road narrow, and with only a few finding it? Isn't Christianity supposed to be "everyone is welcome?" This sounds like an exclusive club where only a select few find the way, are asked to be members, and then allowed inside. Wasn't heaven supposed to be inclusive, not exclusive? Besides that, some even believe the membership list has already been pre-determined and the rest of us are just wasting our time. Can this be explained in the Bible?

SCRIPTURE REFERENCES

"And without faith it is impossible to please God, because anyone who comes to him must believe that he exists and that he rewards those who earnestly seek him" (Hebrews 11:6, NIV).

"This is the verdict: Light has come into the world, but men loved darkness instead of light because their deeds were evil. Everyone who does evil hates the light, and will not come into the light for fear that his deeds will be exposed. But whoever lives by the truth comes into the light, so that it may be seen plainly that what he has done has been done through God" (John 3:19–21, NIV).

"All those the Father gives me will come to me, and whoever comes to me I will never drive away. For I have come down from heaven not to do my will but to do the will of him who sent me" (John 6:37–38, NIV).

"And this is the will of him who sent me, that I shall lose none of all those he has given me, but raise them up at the last day. For my Father's will is that everyone who looks to the Son and believes in him shall have eternal life, and I will raise them up at the last day" (John 6:39–40, NIV).

"Blessed is the man who listens to me, watching daily at my gates, waiting at my doorway. For whoever finds me finds life and receives favor from the Lord. But whoever fails to find me harms himself; all who hate me love death" (Proverbs 8:34, NIV).

- Hebrews 11:6 *"Anyone* who comes to him must believe."

- John 3:21 *"Whoever* lives by the truth."

- John 6:37 *"Whoever* comes to me."

- John 6:40 *"Everyone* who looks to the Son."

- Proverbs 8:34 *"Whoever* finds me finds life."

*Anyone. . .whoever. . .everyone. . .*this sounds very welcoming and inclusive to me. The previous Scriptures are only a few of the countless ways God invites us to come to Him. From cover to cover, the Bible paints a vivid picture of our heavenly Father with His arms open wide and pleading for us to come to Him!

What a beautiful display of the purest and deepest Love known to man! This is not merely a sampling of a shallow, surface type love (represented in many woke denominations that have gone "Christianity lite"), or through eastern/new age spirituality that might possibly be attained through a lifetime of jumping through hoops of works and good deeds. Our heavenly Father is the actual *Source* of all LOVE readily given to anyone willing to choose God's only Son, Jesus. The laws of God and the Ten Commandments were given to steer us in the right direction. Jesus came to earth to become the complete fulfillment of the law and to give us full access to our Heavenly Father's love.

> "FOR CHRIST HAS ALREADY ACCOMPLISHED THE PURPOSE FOR WHICH THE LAW WAS GIVEN. AS A RESULT, ALL WHO BELIEVE IN HIM ARE MADE RIGHT WITH GOD."
>
> —ROMANS 10:4, NLT

THE PARABLE OF
THE WEDDING BANQUET

A king never displays his priceless treasures carelessly, giving easy access to those whose intentions would be dishonorable. He carefully surrounds his treasury with added security to protect it from falling into the wrong hands. So it is with the King of Kings. God's most precious gifts that He longs to give to His children are buried in the treasure chest of His Holy Word.

*The letter of Scripture is a veil just as
much as it is a revelation; hiding while it reveals,
and yet revealing while it hides.*
—ANDREW JUKES,
Theologian

The Bible is full of priceless treasure—hidden within God's laws, commandments, parables, principles, and promises. Reading God's Word is the road map that leads to this treasure and faith is the key that unlocks it. Having *faith in God's Word* is the only way this will happen. Our Heavenly Father longs for His children to discover the divine gifts He has for those who accept His Son Jesus as their Lord and Savior and choose to walk in obedience to His Word.

"Jesus spoke to them again in parables, saying:

"The kingdom of heaven is like a king who prepared a wedding banquet for his son. He sent his servants to those who had been invited to the banquet to tell them to come, but they refused to come. Then he sent some more servants and said, "Tell those who have been invited that I have prepared my dinner: My oxen and fattened cattle have been butchered, and everything is ready. Come to the wedding banquet." But they paid no attention and went off—one to his field, another to his business. The rest seized his servants, mistreated them and killed them. The king was enraged. He sent his army and destroyed those murderers and burned their city. Then he said to his servants, 'The wedding banquet is ready, but those I invited did not deserve to come. So go to the street corners and invite to the banquet anyone you find. So the servants went out into the streets and gathered all the people they could find, the bad as well as the good, and the wedding hall was filled with guests. But when the king came in to see the guests, he noticed a man there who was not wearing wedding clothes. He asked, 'How did you get in here without wedding clothes, friend?' The man was speechless. "Then the king told the attendants, 'Tie him hand and foot, and throw him outside, into the darkness, where there will be weeping and gnashing of teeth.' "For many are invited, but few are chosen" (Mathew 22:1–14, NIV).

The king in the parable made his invitation available to *anyone* who would receive it. He didn't force anyone to come, nor did he allow anyone to stay who dishonored him. The king wanted his invitation to be accepted but for the right reasons. Our King of Kings sees the heart of every man and woman and rightly judges what He finds.

"Who may ascend into the hill of the Lord? Or who may stand in His holy place? He who has clean hands and a pure heart, Who has not lifted up his soul to an idol, Nor sworn deceitfully. He shall receive blessing from the Lord, And righteousness from the God of his salvation" (Psalm 24:3-5, NKJV).

The Bible tells us that before the end of time, the gospel of Jesus Christ will be preached and spread throughout the whole world. America has, for centuries, sent out missionaries to less prosperous nations. However, our nation has fallen into such spiritual decline, that missionaries are now being sent from these same countries to minister to America.

CHRISTIAN PERSECUTION

Christian watchdog organizations report that more believers in Christ have been martyred around the world in the last 100 years, than in all the years combined since Jesus walked the earth. Millions of **Christians** are being slaughtered, especially in Muslim, Communist, and third world countries, under the guise of ethnic cleansing and cultural wars. In the Middle East, the majority of the persecution is motivated by radical Islamic jihad against Christians and Jews, and horrific accounts of mass slaughters are consistently not reported by the liberal press.

The fact that Americans are for the most part unaware of these atrocities, which occur daily around the world, doesn't speak well for this country's liberal press. Lee Webb, a well-known Christian reporter working for the Christian Broadcasting Network over two decades ago said, "The bias of the American liberal press isn't so much in what they report, but in what they don't report!" Sadly, that statement is even more true today as we're beginning to see and experience open hostility toward Christianity and anything that the Bible stands for.

In this era of the proliferation of new age (Eastern) religions and post-modern relativistic thinking, the philosophy *de jour* seems to be "All roads lead to God." The pendulum of public opinion swings wide, from the politically correct, blinded and deceived far left "woke" to the opposite side being "fully awake" and walking in the light of God's Truth. The majority of woke *followers* (which are being used as a propaganda arm for Communism) are being fed deceptive and outright false information that is demonically fueled by those that hate, divide, and destroy. Anything of God is considered an enemy to the left. The Word of God and especially anyone who *obeys* the Word of God and His divine plan for His children, is a threat to their lifestyle of open rebellion against God.

Yet, the masses blindly swallow whatever the radically liberal celebrities, athletes, mainstream media, entertainment talk show hosts, reality TV shows, sit-coms, progressive social media sites, and, sadly, even some anti-Biblical mega-church ministers would have them believe. Only those who *seek* the truth of God for themselves will find the Truth that our loving Heavenly Father and Creator of the Universe has for His obedient children.

THE NARROW ROAD LEADS TO LIFE

"For I know the plans I have for you," declares the Lord, "plans to prosper you and not to harm you, plans to give you hope and a future. Then you will call upon me and come and pray to me, and I will listen to you. You will seek me and find me when you seek me with all your heart. I will be found by you," declares the Lord, "and will bring you back from captivity" (Jeremiah 29:11, NIV).

The statement, "All roads lead to God," is true if each of these roads intersect with Jesus Christ. For the one true God of the universe has a Son named Jesus who willingly died for the sins of the world and rose again to give us eternal life. The traveler will arrive at their ultimate eternal destination in heaven, if they've *chosen* to accept the free gift of Salvation, through the genuine repentance for their sins, and receiving Jesus into their heart that's been cleansed by His blood. Scripture clearly states that unless the road you're traveling leads to Jesus the only Son of God, it ends up being a toll road and exacts the costly penalty of eternity apart from God, which the Bible defines as Hell.

"Jesus answered, "I am the way and the truth and the life. No one comes to the Father except through me" (John 14:6, NIV).

Society bristles at such absolutism. Many say, how could believers in Jesus Christ be so arrogant to think Christianity corners the market on Salvation? Who do they think they are, suggesting I'm on the wrong road! This virulent response, unfortunately, exposes not only the rebellion in their hearts and the lies they believe, but the distance they have placed between themselves and God.

Blaming believers in Christ for embracing Jesus as their Lord and Savior and believing the Truth they've found in the Bible, is easier than honestly saying, "I don't *believe* in Jesus, I don't *believe* the Bible is the inspired Word of God, and I'm *choosing* to travel any road other than the narrow road!" This narrative quickly collapses, however, when confronted with the life-changing, soul transforming, heart melting love of Jesus, who took our place on the cross, giving His Life for ours.

WHICH ROAD WILL YOU CHOOSE?

Pray this prayer:

Heavenly Father, I thank You for giving Your children a way back to You and the divine destiny for which we were created. I choose the narrow road that leads me to Jesus Christ, Your only Son, the King of Kings, and Lord of Lords. Jesus, I repent and ask You to come into my heart and cleanse me of all my sins. Thank You for washing me white as snow with the blood You shed on the cross in my place, to purchase my Salvation, my healing, and my deliverance from every bondage. You took my sinful debt and marked it PAID IN FULL. Thank You for throwing my sins into the Sea of Forgetfulness, never to be remembered again. I thank You Jesus that You rose from the dead so that I might have eternal life and be filled with Your precious Holy Spirit. I give You complete control of my life to fill me, to guide me, and to empower me for the journey ahead.

Jesus, I choose to follow You on the narrow road until You return for Your Bride, the faithful, blood-washed Believers in Christ. In Jesus' Name, Amen.

YOU'RE A NEW PERSON IN CHRIST

"This means that anyone who belongs to Christ has become a new person. The old life is gone; a new life has begun!" (2 Corinthians 5:17, NLT).

Let me know if you have just prayed the prayer of repentance, accepted Jesus into your heart, and have become a new person in Christ! I would love to hear about your *love story* **with the King of Kings, Lord of Lords, True Messiah, and Savior of the world!**

Contact me: Divine Origin Press

P.O. Box 3440 / Grapevine, Texas 76099

DLBollinger@DivineOriginPress.com

www.RabbitTrailsRedirect.com

FROM COVER TO COVER,
THE BIBLE PAINTS A
VIVID PICTURE OF OUR
HEAVENLY FATHER WITH
HIS ARMS OPEN WIDE
AND PLEADING FOR
US TO COME TO HIM!

TALK TO GOD THROUGH HIS WORD

Do not be anxious about anything,
but in every situation, by prayer and petition,
with thanksgiving, present your requests to God.
And the peace of God, which transcends all
understanding, will guard your hearts and your
minds in Christ Jesus. (Philippians 4:6-7 NIV)

PRAYER REQUESTS   **ANSWERED PRAYER**

_____

_____

_____

_____

_____

_____

_____

_____

_____

_____

_____

_____

_____

_____

_____

_____

_____

_____

PRAYER REQUESTS　　　　　　　　**ANSWERED PRAYER**

PRAYER REQUESTS

ANSWERED PRAYER

ENDNOTES

1   Joni Lamb's "Table Talk Show" transcript, interview with Todd White, *The End Of Yourself,* (June 3, 2021).

2   Dutch Sheets, "Keys to Revival," transcript taken from *Give Him 15* daily devotional (March 6, 2023).

3   Dr. Michael Brown (askdrbrown.org) host, nationally syndicated "Line of Fire" radio, book *The Political Seduction of the Church: How Millions of American Christians Have Confused Politics with the Gospel.*

4   Kelly Shackelford, President/CEO First Liberty Institute, *The Survey of Hostility to Religion in America,* (2017 EDITION). https://firstliberty.org › uploadsPDF

5   Dutch Sheets, "Simplicity," transcript taken from *Give Him 15* daily devotional (March 29, 2022)

6   Christopher Reeve, *Reader's Digest* interview (October 2004)

7   Steven R. Weisman, "The Rockefellers," *New York Times,* (Mar 28, 1976). nytimes.com/1976/03/28/archives/the-rockefellers.html

8   Thomas P. Duffy, "The Flexner Report—100 Years Later,"
    Yale Journal of Biological Medicine, (Sep. 2011). ncbi.nlm.
    nih.gov/pmc/articles/PMC3178858/

9   Nigel Chiwaya & Jiachuan Wu, "Unemployment claims
    by state: See how COVID-19 has destroyed the job
    market," *NBC News*, (Apr. 14, 2020, updated Aug. 27,
    2020). https://www.nbcnews.com/business/economy/
    unemployment-claims-state-see-how-covid-19-has-
    destroyed-job-n1183686

10 The Rockefeller Foundation and Global Business
    Network, "Scenarios for the Future of Technology
    and International Development," (May 2010). https://
    nommeraadio.ee/meedia/pdf/RRS/Rockefeller%20
    Foundation.pdf

11 Stella Immanuel, MD, *Let America Live: Exposing
    the Hidden Agenda Behind the 2020 Pandemic—
    My Journey*, Chapter 1, (Charisma House, 2021).

12 Jerry Dunleavy, "Fauci Worked Behind the Scenes to
    Cast Doubt on Wuhan Lab Leak Hypothesis, Emails
    Show," *Washington Examiner*, (June 2, 2021). https://
    washingtonexaminer.com/news/fauci-worked-behind-
    scenes-cast-doubt-wuhan-lab-leak-hypothesis

13   Tucker Carlson, "Tucker: Fauci deserves to be under
     'criminal investigation,'" *Tucker Carlson Tonight*, (June 2,
     2021). youtube.com/watch?v=yp6btJhS66c&t=154s

14   Bill Moyers, "H5N1—Killer Flu—Interview: Dr. Anthony
     Fauci," *PBS—Wide Angle*, (Sep. 20, 2005). pbs.org/
     wnet/wideangle/interactives-extras/interviews/h5n1-
     killer-flu-dr-anthony-fauci/2519/

15   Stuffaford, A., "The Great Reset: If Only It Were Just a
     Conspiracy." *National Review*, (Nov. 27, 2020). https://
     www.nationalreview.com/2020/11/the-great-reset-if-
     only-it-were-just-a-conspiracy/

16   Bill Gates, "Innovating to Zero!," *TED Talk* 4:33, (Feb.
     2010). ted.com/talks/bill_gates_innovating_to_zero

17   Neil Foster, "The Money, the Power and Insanity of Bill
     Gates—The Planned Parenthood Depopulation Agenda,"
     Sovereign Independent UK, (Jan. 31, 2013). http://adam.
     curry.com/art/1380297046_Au563ZWf.html

18   Margaret Sanger, *The Pivot of Civilization In Historical
     Perspective* (Seattle: Inkling Books, 2001), 259.

19   Margaret Sanger, *The Pivot of Civilization:* "Chap5—
     The Cruelty of Charity" (Project Gutenberg, 2008).
     https://gutenberg.org/files/1689/1689-h/1689-h.
     htm#link2HCH0005

20   Prince Philip, Duke of Edinburgh, *The Guardian*, (2009)

21   Nina Federoff, Clinton Advisor: "Earth's Population Has
     Exceeded Limits," *BBC—One Planet*

22   Taro Aso, "Justin McCurry in Tokyo," *The Guardian*, (Jan
     22, 2013)

23   John P. Holdren, Textbook 1977, Ecoscience, population
     control.

24   Margaret Sanger, *Woman and the New Race*, Chapter 5:
     The Wickedness of Creating Large Families (1920)

25   Tanya L. Green, "The NEGRO PROJECT: Margaret
     Sanger's EUGENIC Plan for Black America," *Black
     Genocide*, (2012). http://blackgenocide.org/archived_
     articles/negro.html

26   Pentti Linkola, *The Wall Street Journal Europe,* (May
     1994)

27 Jacques Cousteau, "Environment and development: a global commitment," *The UNESCO Courier*, (Nov. 1991)

28 David Brower, "Trashing the Planet and Environmental Overkill," *Dixy Lee Ray*

29 Ruth Bader Ginsburg, "Supreme Court Harris v. McRae, Life Legal Defense Foundation MN," *New York Times*, (1980)

30 David Turner, "Foundations of Holocaust: American eugenics and the Nazi connection," *Jerusalem Post*, (Dec. 30, 2012). https://www.jpost.com/blogs/the-jewish-problem---from-anti-judaism-to-anti-semitism/foundations-of-holocaust-american-eugenics-and-the-nazi-connection-364998

31 Edwin Black, "Hitler's Debt to America," an excerpt from War Against the Weak: Eugenics and America's Campaign to Create a Master Race, *The Guardian*, (Feb. 5, 2004), https://theguardian.com/uk/2004/feb/06/race.usa

32 Klaus Schwab, "United Nations Department of Economic and Social Affairs, Transforming our world: the 2030 Agenda for Sustainable Development"

33 Klaus Schwab interview, "Microchipping Goal Timeline 2026," (Jan. 10, 2016)

34 Andrzejewski, A., "NIH Scientists Pocketed $350 Million in Royalties—Agency Won't How Much Went to Fauci." *The Defender*, (May 10, 2022). https://childrenshealthdefense.org/defender/nih-scientists-millions-royalties/

35 Rayner, G., "Use of fear to control behaviour in Covid crisis was 'totalitarian', admit scientists." *The Telegraph*, (May 14, 2021). https://www.telegraph.co.uk/news/2021/05/14/scientists-admit-totalitarian-use-fear-control-behaviour-covid/

36 Yale, "COVID-19 Vaccine Messaging, Part 1," ClinicalTrials.gov—sponsored by Yale University, (Jul. 7, 2020). https://clinicaltrials.gov/ct2/show/NCT04460703/

37 Alexis Baden-Mayer, "Dr. Robert Kadlec: How the Czar of Biowarfare Funnels Billions to Friends in the Vaccine Industry," *Organic Consumers*, (Aug. 13, 2020). https://organicconsumers.org/blog/dr-robert-kadlec-how-czar-biowarfare-funnels-billions-friends-vaccine-industry

38 Emily Jacobs, "CNN staffer tells Project Veritas, network played up COVID-19 death toll for ratings," *New York Post*, (Apr. 14, 2021). https://nypost.com/2021/04/14/cnn-staffer-tells-project-veritas-network-played-up-covid-19-death-toll-for-ratings/

39 USFDA, "Emergency Use Authorization of Medical Products and Related Authorities," *U.S. Food & Drug Administration*, (Jan 2017). https://www.fda.gov/regulatory-information/search-fda-guidance-documents/emergency-use-authorization-medical-products-and-related-authorities#preeua.

40 Peter A. McCullough, et al., "Multifaceted highly targeted sequential multidrug treatment of early ambulatory high-risk SARS-CoV-2 infection (COVID-19)," 30;21(4):517-530 Rev Cardiovasc Med. (Dec. 2020), doi: 10.31083/j.rcm.2020.04.264, https://pubmed.ncbi.nlm.nih.gov/33387997/

41 R. Derwanda, M. Scholzb, & V. Zelenko, "COVID-19 outpatients: early risk-stratified treatment with zinc plus low-dose hydroxychloroquine and azithromycin: a retrospective case series study," *International Journal of Antimicrobial Agents*, Volume 56, Issue 6, (Dec. 2020). https://doi.org/10.1016/j.ijantimicag.2020.106214, https://www.sciencedirect.com/science/article/pii/S0924857920304258

42   Monash University, "Lab experiments show anti-parasitic drug, Ivermectin, eliminates SARS-CoV-2 in cells in 48 hours." *Monash Biomedicine Discovery Institute*, (April 3, 2020). https://www.monash.edu/discovery-institute/news-and-events/news/2020-articles/Lab-experiments-show-anti-parasitic-drug,-Ivermectin,-eliminates-SARS-CoV-2-in-cells-in-48-hours

43   AD Santin, et al., "Ivermectin: a multifaceted drug of Nobel prize-honoured distinction with indicated efficacy against a new global scourge," 43:100924 *New Microbes New Infect* (Aug. 3, 2021) doi: 10.1016/j.nmni.2021.100924, https://pubmed.ncbi.nlm.nih.gov/34466270/

44   Rogan, J., "#1757 – Dr. Robert Malone, MD," *The Joe Rogan Experience*, J. Rogan, Editor. (Spotify, 2021). https://open.spotify.com/episode/3SCsueX2bZdbEzRtKOCEyT

45   Wolin, S.S., *Democracy Incorporated: Managed Democracy and the Specter of Inverted Totalitarianism*, (Princeton University Press, 2017), 400.

46   Robert F. Kennedy Jr., "Foreword," Kent Heckenlively and Judy Mikovits, *Plague of Corruption*. (Skyhorse, 2020).

47 Neville Hodgkinson, "Covid's Dark Winter: How Biological War Games Stole Our Freedom," *Conservative Woman* (June 30, 2021). https://conservativewoman. co.uk/covids-dark-winter-how-bio-war-gaming-robbed-us-of-our-liberty/

48 Winters, N., "Exclusive: Deleted Web Pages Show Obama Led an Effort To Build a Ukraine-Based BioLab Handling 'Especially Dangerous Pathogens'," *The National Pulse*, (Mar. 8, 2022). https://thenationalpulse. com/2022/03/08/obama-led-ukraine-biolab-efforts/

49 Adl-Tabatabai, S. "US Embassy Quietly Deletes All Ukraine Bioweapons Lab Documents Online — Media Blackout," *News Punch*, (Feb. 26, 2022). https:// newspunch.com/us-embassy-quietly-deletes-all-ukraine-bioweapon-lab-documents-online-media-blackout/

50 Reality Check Team, "Coronavirus: Was US money used to fund risky research in China?," *BBC* (Aug. 2, 2021). https://www.bbc.com/news/57932699/

51 John Stone, "British Prime Minister Channels Churchill as He Surrenders to Gates and the Vaccine Cartel," *Age of Autism*, (Jun. 5, 2020). https://www.ageofautism. com/2020/06/british-prime-minister-channels-churchill-as-he-surrenders-to-gates-and-the-vaccine-cartel.html

52   Malone, R.W., and J. Glasspool-Malone, "The World
     Economic Forum Young Leaders Program has over
     3800 graduates." *The Malone Institute*, 2022. https://
     maloneinstitute.org/wef

53   Mercola, J., "Who Owns Big Pharma + Big Media?
     You'll Never Guess." *The Defender*, 2021. https://
     childrenshealthdefense.org/defender/blackrock-
     vanguard-own-big-pharma-media/

54   Stuffaford, A., "A Useful Pandemic: Davos Launches
     New 'Reset,' this Time on the Back of COVID."
     National Review, 2020. https://www.nationalreview.
     com/2020/10/a-useful-pandemic-davos-launches-new-
     reset-this-time-on-the-back-of-covid/

55   Charles Ortleb, *Fauci: The Bernie Madoff of Science
     and the HIV Ponzi scheme that Concealed the Chronic
     Fatigue Syndrome Epidemic*, (HHV-6 University Press,
     2020), 27, 39, 41

56   Conor Skelding, "Fauci email dump includes 'sick' March
     Madness-style virus bracket," *New York Post*, (Jun.
     5, 2021). https://nypost.com/2021/06/05/fauci-files-
     include-sick-march-madness-style-virus-bracket/

57   John Lauritsen, T*he AIDS War: Propaganda, Profiteering
     and Genocide from the Medical-Industrial Complex*,
     (Asklepios, 1993), 322

58   Malone, R.W., "'We the people, demand to see the data!
     CDC withholding evidence concerning COVID vaccine
     safety is scientific fraud.," (In Substack @ rwmalonemd,
     2022). https://rwmalonemd.substack.com/p/we-the-
     people-demand-to-see-the-data?utm_source=url

59   John Fund, "'Professor Lockdown' modeler resigns
     in Disgrace," *National Review*, (May 6, 2020). https://
     nationalreview.com/corner/professor-lockdown-
     modeler-resigns-in-disgrace/

60   Tiana Lowe, "Fauci lies about lying about the efficacy
     of masks," *Washington Examiner* (Jun. 21, 2021). https://
     www.washingtonexaminer.com/opinion/fauci-lies-
     about-lying-about-the-efficacy-of-masks

61   Darragh Roche, "Fauci Said Masks 'Not Really Effective
     in Keeping Out Virus,' Email Reveals," *Newsweek* (Jun.
     2, 2021). https://www.newsweek.com/fauci-said-
     masks-not-really-effective-keeping-out-virus-email-
     reveals-1596703

62   Gabby Landsverk, "Long-term quarantines can weaken
     your immune system due to loneliness and stress. Here's
     how to cope," *Insider* (May 12, 2020). https://www.
     insider.com/staying-inside-could-weaken-the-immune-
     system-from-stress-loneliness-2020-5

63 APA, "Stress effects on the body," *American Psychological Association*, (Feb. 26, 2006). https://www.apa.org/topics/stress/body

64 Amy Novotney, "The Risks of Social Isolation," *Monitor on Psychology*, Volume 50, No. 5 (May 2019): 32, https://apa.org/monitor/2019/05/ce-corner-isolation

65 Andrea Germanos, "Big Tech War Profiteers Raked in $44 Billion During 'Global War on Terror,'" *The Defender*, (Sep. 13, 2021). https://childrenshealthdefense.org/defender/big-tech-sells-war-amazon-google-microsoft-44-billion/

66 Allana Aktar, "Pfizer Could Sell Nearly $100 billion Worth of COVID-19 vaccines in the Next Five Years, Morgan Stanley Estimates," *Insider* (May 10, 2021). https://businessinsider.com/pfizer-could-sell-96-billion-dollars-covid-vaccines-morgan-stanley-2021-5?op=1

67 Alexis Baden-Mayer, "Dr. Robert Kadlec: How the Czar of Biowarfare Funnels Billions to Friends in the Vaccine Industry," *Organic Consumers*, (Aug. 13, 2020). https://organicconsumers.org/dr-robert-kadlec-how-czar-biowarfare-funnels-billions-friends-vaccine-industry/

68   Ross Lazarus et al, "Medicare paid hospitals $39,000 per deaths from treating COVID-19, *The Agency for Healthcare Research and Quality*, (Sep. 30, 2010). https:// digital.ahrq.gov/sites/default/files/docs/publication/ r18hs017045-lazarus-final-report-2011.pdf

69   Michelle Rogers, "Fact check: Hospitals get paid more if patients listed as COVID-19, on ventilators— Senator Scott Jensen video," *USA Today*, (Apr. 24, 2020). https://www.usatoday.com/story/news/ factcheck/2020/04/24/fact-check-medicare-hospitals-paid-more-covid-19-patients-coronavirus/3000638001/

70   Alden, M., et al., "Inracellular Reverse Transcription of Pfizer BioNTech COVID-19 mRNA Vaccine BNT162b2 In Vitro in Human Liver Cell Line." *Curr Issues Mol Bill*, (Feb. 25,2022). 44(3): p. 1115-1126. https://www.ncbi.nlm.nih. gov/pubmed/35723296

71   Seneff, S., et al., "Innate immune suppression by SARS-CoV-2 mRNA vaccinations: The role of G-quadruplexes, exosomes, and MicroRNAs." *Food Chem Toxic*, (Jun. 2022). 164: p. 113008. https://www.ncbi.nlm.nih.gov/ pubmed/35436552

72   Trougakos, I.P., et al, "Adverse effects of COVID-19 mRNA vaccines: the spike hypothesis." *Trends Mol Med*, (Apr. 21, 2022). 28(7): p. 542-554. https://www.ncbi.nlm. nih.gov/pubmed/35537987

73 Gram, M.A., et al., Vaccine effectiveness against SARS-COV-2 variant: A nationwide Danish cohort study. *PLoS Med*, (Sep. 2022). 19(9): p. E1003992. https://www.ncbi.nlm.nih.gov/pubmed/36048766

74 Fred Hapgood, "Transhumanism: Securing the Post-Human Future," *CSO* (Jan. 1, 2005). https://csoonline.com/article/2118249/transhumanism--securing-the-post-human-future.html

75 Terry Michael, *Down the Rabbit Hole: How US Medical Bureaucrats, Pharma Crony Capitalists, and Science Literate Journalists Created and Sustain the HIV-AIDS Fraud*, (Unpublished Manuscript), 10

76 Palmer, M., S. Bhakti, and S. Hockertz, "Expert statement regarding Comirnaty—COVID-19-mRNA-Vaccine for children," *Chidren's Health Defense*, (2021). https://childrenshealthdefense.org/wp-content/uploads/expert-evidence-pfizer-children.pdf

77 Sue Halpern, "The Terrifying Potential of the 5G Network," *The New Yorker*, (Apr. 26, 2019). https://www.newyorker.com/news/annals-of-communications/the-terrifying-potential-of-the-5g-network

78 David Rockefeller, "Beware New World Order," Aspen
News, (Aug. 15, 2011). https://www.aspentimes.com/
news/beware-new-world-order/ [Bilderberger Meeting,
Baden Germany, June 1991. Rockefeller has devoted his
life to one world government, i.e. the New World Order
(NWO). He founded the Trilateral Commission and is
integral to the Council on Foreign Relations.]

79 Bill Gates, "Innovating to Zero!," *TED Talk* 4:33, (Feb.
2010). https://ted.com/talks/bill_gates_innovating_to_
zero

80 Meerlooe, J.A.M., *The Rape of the Mind: The Psychology
of Thought Control, Menticide, and Brainwashing.* (2009
ed. 1956: Progressive Press), 326

81 BMGF, "Gates Foundations Give Johns Hopkins $20
Million Gift to School of Public Health for Population,
Reproductive Health Institute," *Bill and Melinda Gates
Foundation*, (May 1999). https://gatesfoundation.org/
ideas/media-center/press-releases/1999/05/johns-
hopkins-university-school-of-public-health

82 Prof. Luc Montagnier, "an interview with Pierre
Barnérias," *Hold-Up Media*

83 John Stone, "Promotional Healthscares," *BMJ Rapid
Response* (Jun. 28, 2007). https://bmj.com/rapid-
response/2011/11/01/promotional-healthscares

84   Nina Shirt et al., "Nosocomial outbreak caused by
     the SARS-CoV-2 Delta variant in a highly vaccinated
     population, Israel, July 2021," *Eurosurveillance*,
     Volume 26, Issue 39, (Sep. 30, 2021). https://www.
     eurosurveillance.org/content/10.2807/1560-7917.
     ES.2021.26.39.2100822

85   Mike Adams, "Finance, climate, diplomacy, science,
     medicine, education and psychology: The "experts" are
     WRONG about almost everything," *Natural News*, (Jun.
     8, 2022). https://www.naturalnews.com/2022-06-08-
     the-experts-are-wrong-about-almost-everything.html

86   Chase Petersen-Withorn, "How Much Money
     America's Billionaires Have Made During the Covid-19
     Pandemic," *Forbes* (Apr. 30, 2021). https://www.
     forbes.com/sites/chasewithorn/2021/04/30/american-
     billionaires-have-gotten-12-trillion-richer-during-the-
     pandemic/?sh=461b1067f557

87   Samuel Stebbins and Grant Suneson, "Jeff Bezos,
     Elon Musk among US billionaires getting richer during
     coronavirus pandemic," USA Today, (Dec 1, 2020).
     https://www.usatoday.com/story/money/2020/12/01/
     american-billionaires-that-got-richer-during-
     covid/43205617/

88 "Viral Inequity: Billionaires Gained $3.9tn, Workers Lost $3.7tn in 2020," *TRT World*, (Jan. 28, 2021). https://www.trtworld.com/magazine/viral-inequality-billionaires-gained-3-9tn-workers-lost-3-7tn-in-2020-43674

89 Leslie E. Sekerka & Lauren, "Thick as Thieves? Big Pharma Wields Its Power with the Help of Government Regulations," *Emory Law Scholarly Commons*, Vol. 5, Issue 2 (2018). https://scholarlycommons.law.emory.edu/ecgar/vol5/iss2/4/

90 Richard Neustadt and Harvey Fineberg, *The Swine Flu Affair: Decision-Making on a Slippery Disease: Swine Flue Chronology January 1976—March 1977*, National Academies Press, (1978). https://ncbi.nlm.nih.gov/books/NBK219595/

91 Redshaw, M., "31,470 Deaths After COVID Vaccines Reported to VAERS, Including 26 Following New Boosters," *The Defender*, (Oct. 14, 2022). https://childrenshealthdefense.org/defender/vaers-deaths-covid-vaccines-boosters/

92 Vera Sharav, "Nobody Should Volunteer for Clinical Trials As Long As Research Data Is Secret," *Alliance for Human Reasearch Protection*, (Apr. 12, 2012). https://ahrp.org/nobody-should-volunteer-for-clinical-trials-as-long-as-research-data-is-secret/

93   Sinopeg, "Polyethylene glycol [PEG] 2000 dimyristoyl glycerol [DMG] [mPEG2000-DMG] Cas:160743-62-4", *SINOPEG:* manufacturer of PEG, (2022). https://www.sinopeg.com/polyethylene-glycol-peg-2000-dimyristoyl-glycerol-dmg-mpeg2000-dmg-cas-160743-62-4_p479.html/

94   Cayman, "Trade name: SM-102, Safety Data Sheet," *Cayman Chemical*, (Jun. 7, 2022). https://cdn.caymanchem.com/cdn/msds/33474m.pdf

95   Cayman, "Trade name: ALC-0315, Safety Data Sheet," *Cayman Chemical*, (Jun. 7, 2022). https://cdn.caymanchem.com/cdn/msds/34337m.pdf

96   Tapp, T., "Newsom Tests Positive for Covid Just 10 Days After His Second Booster Shot," *Deadline*, (May 28, 2022). https://deadline.com/2022/05/gavin-newsom-positive-covid-1235035122/

97   Emmons, L., "AP Source who 'fact checked' Mass Formation Psychosis theory encouraged 'behavioral nudging' people into Covid compliance, quoted Goebbels," *PM*, (Jan. 10, 2022). https://thepostmillennial.com/ap-writer-fact-checked-mass-formation-psychosis-theory-encouraged-cajoling-covid-compliance

98 Rogan, J., "#1757 – Dr. Robert Malone, MD,"
    The Joe Rogan Experience, J. Rogan, Editor.
    (Spotify, 2021). https://open.spotify.com/
    episode/3SCsueX2bZdbEzRtKOCEyT

99 Stuffaford, A., "A Useful Pandemic: Davos Launches
    New 'Reset,' this Time on the Back of COVID." *National
    Review*, (Oct. 29, 2020). https://www.nationalreview.
    com/2020/10/a-useful-pandemic-davos-launches-new-
    reset-this-time-on-the-back-of-covid/

100 "Could Goldman Sachs Report Be Exposing
    Pharma's Real End Game of Drug Dependency
    vs. Curing Disease," *CHD* (Apr. 18, 2018). https://
    childrenshealthdefense.org/news/could-goldman-sachs-
    report-be-exposing-pharmas-real-end-game-of-drug-
    dependency-vs-curing-disease/

101 Teresa Carr, "Too Many Meds? America's Love Affair with
    Prescription Medication," *Consumer Reports*, (Aug. 3,
    2017). https://www.consumerreports.org/prescription-
    drugs/too-many-meds-americas-love-affair-with-
    prescription-medication/#nation

102 Peter C. Gøtzsche, "Prescription drugs are the third
    leading cause of death," *The BMJ Opinion*, (Jun. 16,
    2016). https://blogs.bmj.com/bmj/2016/06/16/peter-
    c-gotzsche-prescription-drugs-are-the-third-leading-
    cause-of-death/

103 Adolph Eichmann quote, "Larry Tomczak: How to Avoid Satan's Crafty Deception," *Charisma News*, (Oct. 14, 2021). https://www.charismanews.com/culture/87075-larry-tomczak-how-to-avoid-satan-s-crafty-deception

104 Dr. Joseph Mercola, "How CDC Manipulated Data to Create 'Pandemic of the Unvaxxed' Narrative," *The Defender*, (Aug. 16, 2021). https://childrenshealthdefense.org/defender/cdc-manipulated-data-create-pandemic-unvaxxed-narrative/

105 Brian Shilhavy, "Attorney Files Lawsuit Against CDC Based on "Sworn Declaration" from Whistleblower Claiming 45,000 Deaths are Reported to VAERS – All Within 3 Days of COVID-19 Shots," *Health Impact News*, (Jul. 19, 2021). https://healthimpactnews.com/2021/attorney-files-lawsuit-against-cdc-based-on-sworn-declaration-from-whistleblower-claiming-45000-deaths-are-reported-to-vaers-all-within-3-days-of-covid-19-shots/

106 William Vinson, "19 Shocking Facts And Theories About The Bilderberg Group", *The Clever*, (Apr. 26, 2017). https://www.theclever.com/20-shocking-facts-about-the-bilderberg-group/

107 Emmons, L., "AP Source who 'fact checked' Mass Formation Psychosis theory encouraged 'behavioral nudging' people into Covid compliance, quoted Goebbels," *PM*, (Jan. 10, 2022). https://thepostmillennial.com/ap-writer-fact-checked-mass-formation-psychosis-theory-encouraged-cajoling-covid-compliance

108 Joel Smalley, "COVID Deaths Before and After Vaccination Programs," YouTube, (2021). https://www.youtube.com/watch?v=WR-pqrMWu3E

109 VAERS-Analysis, "VAERS Summary for COVID-19 Vaccines through 4/8/2022," VAERS Analysis, (Apr. 15, 2022). https://vaersanalysis.info/2022/04/15/vaers-summary-for-covid-19-vaccines-through-4-8-2022/

110 Havens, Barrington S., "History of Project Cirrus ABSTRACT: Project Cirrus, initiated February 28, 1947 under Contract W-36-039-sc-32427, requisition EDG 21190." (Jul. 1, 1952). https://apps.dtic.mil/sti/citations/AD0006880

111 Gérard Delépine, "High Recorded Mortality in Countries Categorized as 'Covid-19 Vaccine Champions'," *Freedom of Speech*, (Oct. 1, 2021). https://fos-sa.org/2021/10/01/high-recorded-mortality-in-countries-categorized-as-covid-19-vaccine-champions-increased-hospitalization/

112   TS News Staff, "Population Wide Epidemiological
      Geography Demonstrates Vaccination Doesn't Correlate
      to Reduction in SARS-CoV-2 Infection," *Trial Site News*,
      (Oct. 3, 2021). https://trialsitenews.com/population-
      wide-epidemiological-geography-demonstrates-
      vaccination-doesnt-correlate-to-reduction-in-sars-cov-2-
      infection/

113   David Mark, "What Have Fauci's Friends Been Up To in
      Ukraine?," *Israel Unwired*, (Feb. 27, 2022). https://www.
      israelunwired.com/faucis-friends-bioweapons-ukraine/

114   Sue Hughes, "CVST After COVID-19 Vaccine: New Data
      Confirm High Mortality Rate," *Medscape*, (Sep. 30, 2021).
      https://www.medscape.com/viewarticle/959992#vp_3

115   CHD, "Court Hears CHD's Arguments Against
      Facebook, Zuckerberg and 'Fact Checkers' Lawyers
      for Children's Health Defense await the ruling of Judge
      Susan Illston after defending CHD's lawsuit alleging
      government-sponsored censorship, false disparagement
      and wire fraud." *The Defender*, May 6, 2021. https://
      childrenshealthdefense.org/defender/court-hears-chd-
      arguments-facebook-zuckerberg-fact-checkers/

116   "Facebook Fact-Checkers Secretly Funded by Johnson
      and Johnson," *Vision News* (May 6, 2021). https://www.
      visionnews.online/post/facebook-fact-checkers-secretly-
      funded-by-johnson-and-johnson/

117 Kelly Laco, "Lawsuit filed against Biden, top officials for 'colluding' with Big Tech to censor speech on Hunter, COVID Lawsuit filed against Psaki, Fauci, Mayorkas and other top Biden administration officials," *Fox News*, (May 5, 2022). https://www.foxnews.com/politics/lawsuit-filed-against-biden-top-officials-colluding-big-tech-censor-speech-hunter-covid

118 Carl Bernstein, "The CIA and the Media," *Rolling Stone*, (Oct. 20, 1977). https://www.carlbernstein.com/the-cia-and-the-media-rolling-stone-10-20-1977

119 Brian Shilhavy, "Whistleblower Lawsuit! Government Medicare Data Shows 48,465 DEAD Following COVID Shots—Remdesivir Drug has 25% Death Rate!," *Health Impact News*, (Sep. 28, 2021). https://medicalkidnap.com/2021/09/28/whistleblower-lawsuit-government-medicare-data-shows-48465-dead-following-covid-shots-remdesivir-drug-has-25-death-rate/

120 Vera Sharav, "Medical Journals Complicit in Corruption of Medicine," *Alliance for Human Reasearch Protection*, (Nov. 13, 2010). https://ahrp.org/medical-journals-complicit-in-corruption-of-medicine/

121 Jeremy R. Hammond, "WHO Experimenting on African Children without Informed Consent," *Foreign Policy Journal*, (Mar. 1, 2020). https://foreignpolicyjournal.com/2020/03/01/who-experimenting-on-african-children-without-informed-consent/

122 HHS Commission, "The Belmont Report, Office of the Secretary, Ethical Principles and Guidelines for the Protection of Human Subjects of Research, The National Commission for the Protection of Human Subjects of Biomedical and Behavioral Research," *U.S. Department of Health and Human Services*, (Apr. 18, 1979). https://www.hhs.gov/ohrp/sites/default/files/the-belmont-report-508c_FINAL.pdf

123 WMA General Assembly, "WMA Declaration of Helsinki—Ethical Principles for Medical Research Involving Human Subjects," *World Medical Association*, (Jun. 1964). https://www.wma.net/policies-post/wma-declaration-of-helsinki-ethical-principles-for-medical-research-involving-human-subjects/

124 Mike Adams, "Media pushing "HIV variant" narrative as cover story for vaccine-induced immune system collapse," *Natural News*, (Feb 16, 2022). https://www.naturalnews.com/2022-02-16-media-pushing-hiv-variant-narrative-as-cover-story-for-vaccine-induced-immune-system-collapse.html

125 Brian Shilhavy, "Whistleblower Lawsuit! Government Medicare Data Shows 48,465 DEAD Following COVID Shots—Remdesivir Drug has 25% Death Rate!," *Health Impact News*, (Sep. 28, 2021). https://medicalkidnap.com/2021/09/28/whistleblower-lawsuit-government-medicare-data-shows-48465-dead-following-covid-shots-remdesivir-drug-has-25-death-rate/

126 SOA, "Group Life COVID-19 Mortality Survey Report,"
     SOA *Research Institute*. (Aug. 2022). https://www.
     soa.org/4a368a/globalassets/assets/files/resources/
     research-report/2022/group-life-covid-19-mortality-03-
     2022-report.pdf/

127 Domina Petric, "Who Is Going to Fast Check the Fast
     Checkers?," *ResearchGate*, (2010). https://researchgate.
     net/publication/343962629_Who_is_going_to_Fast_
     Check_the_Fast_Checkers/

128 AFD, "This Virus Has a Cure," *America's Front Line
     Doctors*, (Jul. 27, 2020). https://www.dailymotion.com/
     video/x7vbtzf/

129 New York Times staff, "Nearly One-Third of U.S.
     Coronavirus Deaths Are Linked to Nursing Homes," *New
     York Times*, (Jun. 1, 2021). https://www.nytimes.com/
     interactive/2020/us/coronavirus-nursing-homes.html

130 U.S. Sen. Ron Johnson, "Google/YouTube censor Senate
     hearing on ivermectin and early treatment of Covid-19,"
     Wall Street Journal, (Feb. 2, 2021). https://www.wsj.com/
     articles/youtube-cancels-the-u-s-senate-11612288061

131 Tenbusch, M., et al., "Risk of immunodeficiency virus infection may increase with vaccine-induced immune response," *Journal of Virology*, (Jul. 18, 2012). 86(19): p. 10533-9. https://www.ncbi.nlm.nih.gov/pubmed/22811518

132 Lee, W.S., et al., "Antibody-dependent enhancement and SARS-CoV-2 vaccines and therapies," *Nature Microbiology*, (Sep. 9, 2020). 5(10): p. 1185-1191. https://www.ncbi.nlm.nih.gov/pubmed/32908214

133 Crawford, N., A. Harris, and G. Lewis, "Vaccine-associated enhanced disease (VAED)," *Melbourne Vaccine Education Centre*, (Nov. 29, 2022). https://mvec.mcri.edu.au/references/vaccine-associated-enhanced-disease-vaed/

134 Klaus Schwab, *Covid-19 The Great Reset*, (Agentur Schwei, 2020)

135 Edward Dowd, *Cause Unknown: The Epidemic of Sudden Deaths in 2021 & 2022*, (Skyhorse, 2022)